Soup
wisdom

Soup wisdom

by Frieda Arkin
and the Editors of Consumer Reports Books

Consumers Union, Mount Vernon, New York

Library of Congress Catalog Card Number: 80-68223
International Standard Book Number: 0-89043-018-7
Copyright © 1980 by Frieda Arkin and Consumers Union of United
States, Inc., Mount Vernon, New York 10550
Manufactured in the United States of America
Illustrations by Don Almquist

Soup Wisdom is a Consumer Reports Book published by Consumers Union, the nonprofit organization that publishes CONSUMER REPORTS, the monthly magazine of test reports, product Ratings, and buying guidance. Established in 1936, Consumers Union is chartered under the Not-For-Profit Corporation Law of the State of New York.

The purposes of Consumers Union, as stated in its charter, are to provide consumers with information and counsel on consumer goods and services, to give information on all matters relating to the expenditure of the family income, and to initiate and to cooperate with individual and group efforts seeking to create and maintain decent living standards.

Consumers Union derives its income solely from the sale of CONSUMER REPORTS and other publications. In addition, expenses of occasional public-service efforts may be met, in part, by noncommercial grants and fees. Consumers Union accepts no advertising or product samples and is not beholden in any way to any commercial interest. Its Ratings and product reports are solely for the use of the readers of its publications. Neither the Ratings nor the reports nor any other Consumers Union publications, including this book, may be used in advertising or for any commercial purpose. Consumers Union will take all steps open to it to prevent such uses of its material, its name, or the name of CONSUMER REPORTS.

Contents

Introduction

To introduce you to the wonderful world of soup-making, *Soup Wisdom* offers—as you will see—a new telling of an old legend: "Nail Soup." In some collections of folk tales this story is called "Stone Soup." The fact that a nail is substituted for a stone may be poetic license, but it's also a perfect introduction to soup lore. In soup-making there are always plenty of possibilities for substituting ingredients. One of the nicest things about soup-making is that you don't really have to follow a recipe with precision. *Chacun à son gout.*

Good homemade stock is the basis of good homemade soup. You get more than recipes, however, in the chapter on how to make stocks. You learn which leftovers to save and store for the day when the stock-making spirit takes hold, and how to enrich or vary stock already on hand. And if you want to prepare soup but have no homemade stock, you can find out how to make do with store-bought alternatives.

Turning stock into soup is no alchemist's trick; it's good old-fashioned soup wisdom. With the right combination of solids, thickeners, flavorings, and garnishes, you just may produce liquid gold.

A section on how to use the recipes leads you to the recipes themselves. A cursory glance reveals that they involve a fairly wide range of the kinds of ingredients customarily used in soup-making—although how they are put together is not always the customary way. And some of the recipes—peanut butter soup, caraway soup, and parsnip soup, for example—may strike you as a little unusual.

Now don't let prejudice cripple your sense of daring. After all, a food you're not particularly fond of may, in combination with other foods, produce something new and wonderful. Soup is the fusion of food and seasoning, and seemingly incongruous elements may come together as a positive delight for you—but you won't know unless you experiment.

A chapter on creating your own soup recipes is one of the special features of *Soup Wisdom*. Making up your own soup recipes is a culinary adventure. And the results can be both aesthetically and nutritionally rewarding.

As supermarket shelves attest, a lot of people prepare a lot of soups from cans or from dehydrated soup mixes. For any such soup to come close to the quality of homemade soup, one would have to do a pretty miserable job of making homemade soup. Such store-bought products do offer convenience, true, and they don't require much work: "Simply follow directions on the label." But they also may offer questionable nutritional value. And they can hardly provide the satisfaction that comes from a start-to-finish homemade soup.

Consumers Union has tested canned soups and dehydrated soup mixes, and found most of them a poor substitute for homemade. Reports of those tests, originally published in CONSUMER REPORTS, have been revised especially for inclusion in *Soup Wisdom*. In referring to these chapters, you can't lose: Either they will inspire you more than ever to make your own soups or, if you persist in using the store-bought versions, you will have at least some guidance in how to make the best of it.

Frieda Arkin's introduction to her book *Kitchen Wisdom* states that "discovery is what this book is all about." In *Soup Wisdom* there are also discoveries to be made: the wholesomeness of homemade stocks and soups, the adventure of creating your own soup recipe, and the beautiful satisfaction of thrift.

How the recipes were tested

In addition to being prepared and savored over the years in the kitchen of Frieda Arkin, all the recipes in *Soup Wisdom* have been tested by Consumers Union. First, members of CU's staff were called upon to volunteer to choose one of the recipes and to prepare it in the comfort of their own kitchen. Participating staff members then filled out a report, answering such questions as the type of kitchen range and pot used, the dominant flavor of the soup, whether it was inexpensive to prepare, whether the soup was considered tasty enough to make again, and the like. Their replies (including a few trenchant comments) were taken into consideration by CU's Foods Division when the time came for further testing and tasting of the recipes, which took place in CU's test kitchens.

The lucky staff members who made up CU's informal soup-tasting panel had soup for lunch until the thirty recipes in *Soup Wisdom* were tested. These were "blind" tests in that the participating staff members were told neither the name of the soup they were tasting nor any of the ingredients used. In fact, they were told nothing, simply served a bowl of soup.

They were also given a questionnaire to fill out. In addition to asking them to identify the dominant flavor of the soup, the questionnaire had the tasters check one of seven choices that best summed up their overall reaction to the soup: excellent, very good, good, neutral, fair, poor, unacceptable. Next, they selected from thirty-six descriptive words or phrases listed in four categories—flavor, aroma, texture, and appearance—those that, in their opinion, best described the characteristics of the soup. There was also space for additional comments or opinions.

One question considered early in the planning of the test procedures concerned the use of salt. Soup is one dish that can be cooked without salt, and salt can then be added at the table. The taste for salt varies widely, and when soup is too salty there isn't much one can do about it.

Taste aside, some people—for medical or other reasons—seek to curtail their use of salt. So, CU's Foods Division decided to prepare the soups without salt and to serve them to the tasters with salt on the side. Sure enough, to many of the tasters, many of the soups did not suffer from the absence of salt. And some tasters who added salt to some soups experimentally, even though it wasn't needed, found that salt did not enhance the soup.

All the reports from members of CU's informal soup-tasting panel, including their comments on salt, were then evaluated and the recipes refined. The result of the collaboration of Frieda Arkin and Consumers Union is *Soup Wisdom*.

PART I

Nail soup

Once upon a time there was a woman who lived with her husband, a woodcutter, in a cottage in the middle of a forest. The husband made a good living cutting down trees and selling them for lumber or firewood in the nearby villages.

Late one winter's morning the woman heard a knocking at the cottage door and opened it to discover a young man standing there. He had a jaunty air about him, but his clothes were so tattered that the woman thought at once he'd come for a handout. She and her husband were poor people, she said hastily. They had barely enough to eat themselves. As a matter of fact, that night they'd have less than half a loaf of bread for supper.

"Ah, that means you don't have a bit of a crust to spare a poor hungry fellow," the young man said.

"Indeed not! If we only had the strength, we'd go begging ourselves."

"Oh, you're not to think I'm begging," cried the young man. "Look at what I've got here." And from his pocket he drew a tenpenny nail.

She viewed it suspiciously. "What's that? Looks like a nail to me."

"A nail it is. But it happens to be a magic nail. You've only to drop it into a pot of water, set the pot over the fire, and in a few hours you'll have the most delicious soup in seven kingdoms. All I ask is that you have the kindness to give me the use of a pot of water over your fire so I can make myself a bit of soup."

"Just you let me have a look at that," said the wood-cutter's wife. He placed the nail on her palm. It looked to be an ordinary tenpenny nail—a bit bent, at that. "Are you meaning to tell me that if you put this nail in a pot of water it will make soup?" she asked him.

"Well, the pot has to be over a good roaring fire to begin with. And you might add a pinch of salt, if so be it you like salt in your soup. That's all there is to it."

Her curiosity overcame her caution, and she invited the young man into the cottage.

"Now, just give me a pot of clean, cold water," he told her. She brought out a large cast-iron pot, which he filled with water drawn from the well. Plink! He dropped the nail in. "Now if you'll have the goodness to feed up that fire," he said, "you're going to have such soup as you've never had the good luck to taste in your life before."

The woodcutter's wife marveled, still half-suspicious. "With just a nail?"

"Just a nail. Perhaps a few grains of salt, if you have it."

"Certainly, certainly, what's soup without a pinch of salt!" She opened her cupboard and the young man had a glimpse of well-stocked shelves before he looked hastily away.

"Do you think perhaps a little pepper too?" she asked uncertainly.

"Oh absolutely, a little pepper, if you like your soup peppered, which I personally do."

"And so do I," said she, as she watched him add salt and pepper to the pot of water. She could see tiny bubbles forming around the nail, which appeared to be resting comfortably at the bottom of the pot.

"Now," he said, "here's an excellent opportunity for you to get rid of any old vegetables you might have lying around. A half of onion, perhaps. An aging carrot or two. You know what I mean? Something you might otherwise throw out."

"Why, it happens I do have half an onion waiting for something to be done with it," she said. "And here are a couple of wrinkled carrots, or do you think they'll spoil your soup?"

"Spoil the soup? Not on your life! Wash them and throw them in. Maybe you've some other things lying about. I believe in thrift, you know. Why throw out things when you can make use of them?"

She hurried to the vegetable chest. "Here's a dried-up old parsnip I meant to throw out yesterday. What do you think of it?"

He studied it judiciously. "I'd say, throw it in. My magic nail will handle it. I see you have some celery leaves there. I always think celery leaves add a lot to a soup."

"Oh, I think the same."

"And you know, you might throw in a stray bone or two if you happen to have any," said the young scamp, who had already spied a chicken carcass on the counter top.

In went the chicken carcass.

"It wouldn't kill it, either, if you added half a cup of

wine to it. *If* you happen to have an opened bottle sitting about. Things like that help to make a soup more . . . full-bodied, you might say."

The pot was bubbling merrily, its fragrance filling the room. They spoke companionably of soup, comparing thick soups to thin, hearty soups to delicate. The time flew by and before either of them realized, it was suppertime.

The room smelled heavenly.

"Why, here's my husband, home from work. Now you must sit down with us and have a bowlful of your soup," the woman said to the young man.

They all sat down at the table and she served the soup in brimming bowls with slabs of bread she'd baked that morning and fine creamery butter the woodcutter had brought with him from the village. His wife told him the tale of the soup. Made with a nail—a mere nail—in a potful of water! Her husband marveled and shook his head. What wouldn't they think of next.

The wife, having made up her mind to own the remarkable nail at any cost, told the young man that it was far too late for him to be going through the forest. He might, if he wished, spend the night on a pallet near the fire—an offer that he accepted graciously.

In the morning—so marvelous had the soup been the night before—the woodcutter said he must have another bowl of it before departing for work; and so they all three had more soup. And the nail having reposed in the soup for the whole night made the soup taste even better than it had the day before, they told one another.

When the woodcutter left, his wife turned to the young man. "You must sell me this wonderful nail," she cried passionately. "Never have I tasted such soup as it has made!"

"Exactly what I told you yesterday," he replied gravely. "But I cannot be parted from it. My nail is all that stands between me and starvation."

"But I will give you plenty of silver. Only see," cried the woman, "here is a goodly supply which I keep in my sugar bowl for all those little extras in life." And she poured silver into his cupped hands. "With this you need never be hungry."

She cajoled, she wheedled, and finally she succeeded in getting him to accept the silver for the magic nail.

The young man, pockets jingling, took his leave of her. "Mind you," he called back to her, "don't forget the pinch of salt."

You too can make marvelous soup

And you don't need a nail to make it.

Soup. Minestra. Potage. Sopa. Suppe. A magic word in any language. A bowl of soup should be a statement of warmth and hospitality. Soup is actually easy to make: All you need is some liquid, some solids, some native wit and imagination. It's inexpensive. It can be delicious beyond belief. And it can be full of nutrients. Life could probably be sustained entirely on soup.

The nicest thing about soup-making is that you don't really have to follow a recipe precisely (even though there are recipes in this book). You can use almost any proportions of ingredients as long as you have enough liquid to carry them. The permutations and combinations are infinite, and so is the variety. Start up a pot of soup and you can keep it going for days, adding things from time to time, boiling it up and letting it simmer a little each day.

With a soup pot around you never have to wonder what to do with that odd piece of onion, a couple of leftover slices from a jar of pimientos, one or two carrots, the baked potato you didn't feel like eating. And so on and so on.

A soup pot could be called a universal receiver. One day you can throw in a handful of barley and cook it up gently. On another day, a can of tomatoes. On a third, some split peas. And there's little work to it. Most soups cook quietly and competently while you're doing other things. And there's precious little expense, once you've got the initial pot going.

It's traditional to talk about winter soups and summer soups, but any soup can be a soup for any season. A good rich gumbo makes a marvelous one-dish meal, even in the middle of the summer. And a soup course that precedes a lavish "company dinner," though it be served in the chill of winter, can—and often should—be a delicate consommé.

You can start a soup from scratch, using water, vegetables, bones, meat, and seasoning, and cook it slowly for hours, as one should do for most good soups. Or, you can make the finest of soups much more quickly by using as the base of the liquid portion of the soup some stock you've already prepared. You can also use cans of clear chicken or beef broth or consommé—not as full-flavored as homemade stock, it's true, but still satisfactory soup bases. Keep a few on your pantry shelf.

The stocks

Any soup you make will be mightily influenced by the flavor of your stock. This is as it should be. It's one reason why two soups made from the same recipe are rarely exactly alike. And each variation can be delicious, though delicious in different ways.

It can't be emphasized enough that what makes the soup is the stock you use. Properly rich and full-flavored, stock can be served as is or with nothing more than texture added to it: pieces of meat, vegetables, noodles, thickening. A good stock is a cinch to make and it can be made in quantity and frozen until needed. Having a prepared stock on hand can save you hours of soup-making time.

There are few basic differences among the terms broth, bouillon, consommé, and stock. They are often used interchangeably; but for the record, here are the significant distinctions:

Broth is the same as *bouillon*. Both terms can be used for a clear liquid resulting from the cooking of water with meat (or chicken or fish) and vegetables and seasoning, followed by straining. A broth (or bouillon) can be served as is, with or without a garnish.

Stock is a broth that is used as the base of a more elaborate soup (or sauce or gravy). A stock can be prepared from meat, chicken, or fish.

Consommé is a stock that is enriched by further cooking with meat or chicken, then strained and clarified (see page 29), usually with egg white, and served as soup.

In this chapter there are recipes for a good basic chicken or meat stock and for a fish stock. But it's not always necessary to follow a recipe when you start out to make a chicken or meat stock. Ingredients of such stocks don't have to be planned ahead of time or shopped for in the same deliberate fashion as for many other cooking ventures. A chicken or meat stock can be constituted from materials you've stockpiled ahead of time—things readily available in most kitchens.

Makings for a chicken or meat stock

The inclination to make soup may not be strong some days. But even if you don't feel like making soup right away, you can still contribute to the stock pot. All you have to do is refrigerate chicken or meat and vegetable leavings—even the liquids—and, once they are cooled, transfer them to a large plastic container for storage in the freezer. The day may always come when you're in the mood for making a chicken or meat stock.

Remember, if you want the ingredients for a good chicken or meat stock, save all drippings when you cook chicken or meat dishes. And never throw out any cooked meat, chicken bones, meat bones, or leavings, or even vegetable parings. Toss all such makings, once they've been rapidly cooled by refrigeration, into the collection in your freezer destined for the stock pot. (If space permits, you may want to use one container for meat scraps and another for chicken.)

Meat trimmings that have been cut off before cooking—including bones—can also be saved for the stock pot. Raw chicken trimmings, including bone and skin, can be frozen. Raw chopped peelings from freshly scrubbed vegetables can be put into the blender or food processor with a little liquid and then added to the stock collection. (Potato water is particularly flavorful when added to stock. You never need a lot of water to cook potatoes, but if there's some left over, simmer it down to a manageable amount, refrigerate it, and then add to your soup stock container.) Most of these scraps have some nutrients and they *taste good*.

When the container is full, and you're in the mood to make stock, place the contents in a pot, cover with cold water, add a little salt and other seasoning, set the heat very low, and bring to a simmer. Keep the stock at a simmer for three hours or so. Then strain and refrigerate it, covered, until the fat congeals and can be lifted off. Now you have a chicken or meat stock. Further seasoning can be added now or later—when you use the stock to make a soup.

Once you've prepared a good supply of stock, you can use some to make soup immediately to serve for supper the same day, if you like. The remainder of the stock can be reserved for another day's soup. That way, with stock on hand, it's as though when you start out on a journey you have the good luck to be halfway there at the very beginning of it.

You can make stock days—even a week or more—in advance and still not have to freeze it. Refrigerate the stock, covered, immediately after cooking, preferably in several containers to speed cooling. After the surface of the stock has developed a layer of congealed fat, you can leave the stock in the refrigerator for a week or more before using it. Once you have removed the layer of congealed fat from a container of stock and you don't use all of it immediately, put the remaining stock, covered, back in the refrigerator. Bring it out every three days, heat it to a low rolling boil and cook for 10 minutes. If you do this many times, add a bit more water or, preferably, liquid in which you've cooked vegetables because some of the stock and its nutrients will boil away.

Or you can freeze the stock: Pour into containers, allowing room for expansion, cover, and put in the freezer. (Be sure to label and date containers.) It's a good idea to divide the stock into several portions. Small containers are easier to store in the freezer, freeze quicker, and allow you to defrost only as much as you're likely to need at any one time. Frozen stock will stay good for several months. Freezer temperatures vary, generally speaking, and so your own experience with other foods you have successfully stored in your freezer will suggest how long the stock will stay good.

Suppose you have only a small storage space in your freezer or refrigerator. All that has to be done once the fat is removed is to simmer the stock down very, very slowly until you get what's called a *glaze*: a highly concentrated semiliquid that will take up very little storage space. Then, when you add water to this, and some vegetables, perhaps some bits of leftover chicken or meat, you've got soup. And without a nail!

A stock becomes full-flavored when it's toned up with

special additions. You can always tone up a chicken or
meat stock, regardless of how you made it, by adding
one or more of the following:

> onions, sautéed until very well browned
> 1 beef or chicken bouillon cube (perhaps 2, but never more)
> 1 or more tablespoons tomato paste (for meat stock only)
> soy sauce, Worcestershire sauce, any kind of steak sauce
> ½ cup or so wine (white wine for chicken stock), or a
>   couple of tablespoons brandy
> 1 mashed anchovy (yes, even in a meat or chicken stock)

Chicken or meat stock

There will be times when you won't have collected the
makings for a chicken or meat stock in the freezer and
will have to prepare stock from scratch. To do that,
you'll need to have on hand:

> 4 pounds bones, cut into 4- to 6-inch pieces

For chicken stock, use chicken wings, legs, backs, necks,
etc., as well as chicken carcasses or any bones left over
from cooked chicken. For meat stock, use beef, pork,
veal, or lamb bones with or without meat attached, separately or in any combination, raw or leftovers. Place
the bones in a heavy 7- or 8-quart soup pot (one with
a tight-fitting lid) and add:

> 1 pound onions (no need to peel), washed and quartered
> 1 large carrot, scrubbed, cut into ½-inch slices

Unless the bones have a great deal of fat on them, add:

> 2 tablespoons cooking oil or other fat

Put the pot over moderate heat. Mix everything up well
and cook, uncovered, stirring often, until the bones be-

come well browned and a fine faintly burned aroma fills the air (about 40 minutes). Then add to the pot:

½ cup any wine (white wine for chicken stock)
2 garlic cloves (no need to peel), cut in halves
10 whole peppercorns
1 teaspoon salt

For meat stock only, also add:

2 tomatoes, sliced, or 4 tablespoons tomato paste

Cover the contents with cold water. Bring to a boil, then turn down the heat to a low simmer. Cook, covered, for about 4 hours. Stir now and then to bring up the bones from the bottom. At the end of 4 hours or so, remove the large bones, then strain the liquid into one or more containers, cover, and refrigerate for 6 or more hours. As long as the entire surface has an unbroken layer of congealed fat on it, you can leave the container in the refrigerator for a week or more before you use the stock. Otherwise, cover the stock and every three days heat it to a high boil for 10 minutes.

When you're ready to make soup, or if you intend to freeze the stock, remove any fat in a block from the top of the stock, if the liquid has jelled. Otherwise, pour the liquid slowly through a fine strainer to remove all the congealed fat. This will give you about 3 quarts of stock. You now have a full-flavored fat-free stock that you can use as the base for any number of soups.

If you want to clarify the stock—that is, make the stock clearer—strain it again, cold, through a large white handkerchief, which has been dampened and spread over a strainer. If you want the stock clearer still, as for a clear consommé, beat an egg white plus an eggshell broken into small pieces into each quart of boiling stock.

Then boil for an additional minute or two. Let cool for 30 minutes and strain, as above, through a large white handkerchief. (If you don't use all the stock at one time, store the remainder in the refrigerator or freezer according to the directions on page 29.)

Fish stock

To prepare a fish stock you will need to follow a different procedure than for chicken or meat stock. Put the following ingredients into a heavy 7- or 8-quart soup pot (one with a tight-fitting lid):

> 4 to 5 pounds fish bones and all fish trimmings (try to avoid fatty fish like mackerel)
> 2 quarts cold water
> 1 large onion, peeled and chopped
> 1 tablespoon lemon juice
> 1 cup white wine
> handful fresh parsley
> ½ teaspoon dried thyme leaves
> 1 large bay leaf, crumbled
> 10 whole peppercorns
> 1 teaspoon salt

Bring to a boil. Stir carefully and well, turn heat down to a simmer, cover, and cook for about 30 minutes. Stir at least twice during this period.

Next, remove most of the bones and other solids with a slotted spoon and strain the stock through a fairly coarse strainer. Strain again through a finer strainer, then one last time through cheesecloth or a large white handkerchief, which has been dampened and spread over a strainer.

Pour the strained stock into one or more containers and refrigerate. Be sure you use an airtight cover to keep the aroma from affecting other foods in the refrigerator.

You may need to remove a little surface fat from the cooled and congealed stock, but that will be rare. Use a small pointed spoon for this.

If you don't plan to use the fish stock within two days, it's a good idea to refrigerate it and then freeze it for future use (allow room for expansion).

Enriching and using fish stock

As you can see from the recipe, fish stock, called a *fumet*, is made of fish bones, skin, heads, etc., cooked in water, with many of the same additions as you would use when making other kinds of stock.

Because a fish stock requires such a large quantity of fish parts, it's unlikely that you'll freeze enough fish or seafood leftovers for the purpose of making stock. But what you can do is freeze fish and seafood leftovers to enrich a fish stock you've already made.

Anytime you cook seafood for a meal, strain the liquid into the fish stock (or reserve and freeze to add to a fish stock you intend to make). Strain into the stock, also, the water in which you steam clams, mussels, or oysters. Whenever you cook shrimp for a dish, wash the shells and boil them in a cup or so of water for 10 minutes. Strain this water into the fish stock.

You may want to add a can or a bottle of clam juice to fish stock, perhaps. If you plan to add wine to the stock, keep to white wine.

A fish stock will be richer if you cook a veal knuckle or some pork bones in it. You can also add an anchovy to fish stock; just go easy on adding salt too.

A little sherry or madeira wine makes a fish stock very tasty if you add it just before you use the stock to make a fish soup or chowder.

Turning stock into soup

To help transform a stock into a soup, one or more of the following can be added: solids, thickeners, flavorings, garnishes.

You may want to experiment to see which of the following ingredients will go best with any of the others. It's not often you'll get a *bad* combination, and you may hit on something remarkably good.

Solids

Meats: any cooked leftovers, including chicken or fish, cut into pieces (some finely chopped bacon or ham can be particularly good); lean, raw meat, cut diagonally across the grain into very thin slices.

Vegetables: fresh, frozen, oven-dried, canned, raw, blanched, boiled, or sautéed; or already cooked from a previous dish.

barley
beans
beets and beet greens
broccoli
brussels sprouts

cabbage
carrots
cauliflower
celery and celery leaves
corn
eggplant
garlic
leeks
lentils
lettuce, shredded
mushrooms
onions
parsnips
peas
potatoes
scallions
shallots
spinach
squash
tomatoes
turnips, white or yellow (rutabaga)
zucchini

Thickeners

Many of the solids listed above, when cooked in a stock will thicken a soup. In addition, here are some suggestions for other thickeners.

arrowroot
beans, dried
bread, a slice or two, crustless and finely diced
bread or cracker crumbs
cornstarch

egg yolk
flour
lentils
okra
peas: chick-, green split, or yellow
peanut butter or any finely ground nuts
potatoes (including mashed potatoes)
rice
tomato paste
vegetables, cooked and puréed in a blender or food processor

Flavorings

Here's a list of possible flavorings to have at hand for soup-making. Some of these flavorings come in a can or a jar. If you've had them on your shelf for a while check to make sure they are still tasty and have retained their fragrance.

allspice
bay leaves
butter
cayenne
chili powder
cloves
curry powder
dill, fresh
fennel (especially in fish soups)
garlic
honey or sugar
lemon, orange, or lime rind
mace
nutmeg
nuts, ground

onion, sautéed until well browned, or boiled
parsley
pepper, ground or whole
salt
soy sauce
Tabasco
tomato paste
Worcestershire sauce
other fresh or dried herbs

Garnishes

A garnish gives a fine touch to a bowl of soup: a pleasure to both the eye and the palate.

bacon, cooked and finely crumbled
basil, fresh chopped
hard cheese of any kind, finely grated
chives, minced
cream, whipped (slightly flavored dabs)
croutons
cucumber, sliced thin
dill, finely cut fresh green
dumplings
egg, freshly poached, slipped into a bowl of clear hot soup just before serving
egg threads: beat an egg well with a little water, then pour into an oiled or buttered wide skillet; heat until it co-agulates, then turn out onto a board and cut into threads
ham, cut into long thin strips or well chopped
lemon, very thinly sliced
mushrooms, dried and simmered in seasoned water or broth until soft
nutmeg, grated (especially on a cream soup)

nuts, finely ground

onion, very finely chopped

paprika

parsley, chopped

potatoes, mashed and mixed with an egg yolk and made into tiny balls, then cooked for a couple of minutes in the soup (they rise to the surface when they're done and make an attractive garnish)

scallions, minced

scallion flowers: white stalks of scallions cut in 1½- to 2-inch lengths, then cut lengthwise about ⅓ of the way up from each end; dropped into very cold water, they'll flare out into "flowers" (nice to garnish a consommé or a clear soup with meat or vegetables added)

tomatoes, sliced thin, and broiled

vegetables: any leftover vegetables can be julienned (cut into very fine strips) and used as garnish for a soup

Stock as soup

And lastly here are three quick ways to serve your stock as a soup, with no further cooking:

Cover the bottom of a large serving bowl with slices of toasted French or Italian bread. Cover the toast layer with very thin slices of cheese: Swiss, Gruyère, Fontina, Muenster, any cheese you like. Add another layer of toast and another of cheese. Pour boiling stock over this and set the bowl in a warm oven for 10 minutes. Serve at the table.

Gently crack one or two eggs, taking care not to break the yolks, into each individual serving bowl. Pour enriched boiling stock over the eggs. If the stock is truly boiling, it will poach them. Garnish and serve.

A marvelous way to serve a clear but tasty broth: Set a slice of bread fried in butter (or margarine) in each soup bowl. Pour very hot broth over the bread and serve. This is even better if you cover the bowl lavishly with Parmesan, or other freshly grated cheese.

Random thoughts on soup-making

Unless you use homemade stock for your soup liquid, don't expect a soup to taste its best on the same day you make it. And even a stock-based soup will be improved when served the next day. Most soups not only have to cook very slowly, they need the passage of time to mature and ripen (just as people do).

When you've got a soup going on the stove, shift the pot a little now and then to equalize the heat. You'll find the bottom less likely to burn in one spot. With a really good soup pot, however, this won't be necessary (see page 47).

But you don't have to keep the heat going under the soup pot throughout the day. You'll be surprised at how long soup can cook tranquilly after the heat has been turned off. After the pot's been simmering smartly for a while, stir the soup and scrape the bottom of the pot with a wooden spoon, cover, then turn off the heat, and let the soup stand. It cooks as it cools, and a half-hour or so later you can put the heat on again for a bit.

The next time you use the oven for baking or roasting, slip in a pan of chopped onions or carrot chips, or chopped celery, or sliced mushrooms to dry and toast.

Practically all vegetables can be oven-dried and this gives them a beautiful flavor when they're added to soup. It is also a good way to use up a leftover half of onion or a couple of stray carrots.

You can keep a soup pot going indefinitely, refrigerating it between uses. Remember to take it out every three days, boil it up, cover it, and lower the heat so it simmers steadily for a minimum of 10 minutes. Don't remove the cover before you return the soup pot to the refrigerator. And each time after you serve the soup, simmer the remainder (if any) steadily for another 10 minutes before you store it in the refrigerator.

Soup can become a little dark from continual day-after-day cooking (though the flavor remains great). So when you want to add uncooked vegetables, macaroni, beans, or other solids (see page 33) as a restorative, cook them separately in a little water and when they're tender, add them—and the cooking water—to the soup.

Variety is the spice of soup

Here are some suggestions for enlivening a pot of soup:

Put the entire contents of a can of any kind of vegetable into the blender or food processor, purée, and add to the soup.

Add a dash of Worcestershire sauce. Or any steak sauce you like.

A tablespoon or so of tomato paste lends a fine touch to a meat-based soup.

Add one-half cup of wine. Or you can substitute one-half cup of fruit juice.

Have on hand any of the following to add to your soup: fresh or dried herbs (if dried, pulverize them well between your palms, then drop them into the soup). Fresh or powdered garlic (*lots* of fresh garlic; it becomes sweet as it boils or simmers). A pinch or so of curry powder. A little chili powder.

Toss in some macaroni or spaghetti, broken up. A handful of dried beans or split peas. A little rice. You may need to add more liquid when you include these starchy ingredients.

A bit of sweetening brings magic to a hearty soup. Try a tablespoon of honey. This is one of the reasons why onions, which contain much natural sugar, are one of the prime ingredients in a soup.

Any meat or vegetable sauce or gravy (including small amounts of spaghetti sauce) may be added to the soup pot.

Every now and then sauté some onions, celery, carrots, or fresh tomatoes in butter (or margarine) or cooking oil until they're slightly browned, and add to the soup pot.

PART II

The soups

The soup recipes that follow, complete as they are, can all be modified to suit your own taste.

You can increase the amounts of liquids and solids to serve more people.

You can substitute vegetable juices for meat or chicken stock, should you run short of stock.

Spices and herbs can be altered in kinds and amounts. You can make substitutions among basil, chervil, and parsley, for example, or savory (if you can find it). Dried herbs can be used instead of fresh; remember that you must decrease the amounts of herbs if they are dried.

You can substitute fresh or frozen beans for dried beans. When using fresh or frozen beans increase the amount by one-third.

All of the soups—with the exception of those containing meat, chicken, or pasta—can be puréed and served cold. It's usually necessary to increase the amount of liquid, however, as well as seasoning. Experiment.

You can garnish the soups as your own fancy directs. For example, sprinkle grated cheese or paprika or chopped dill or parsley over a bowl of soup immediately

before serving. Or garnish with chopped egg or croutons.

In short, you can add different ingredients as your
taste and inclinations move you. That's the blessing of
soup: It adjusts happily to your appetite, your imagination, and your larder.

Using the recipes

It's important to read a recipe through to the end before
you start to cook. For one thing, you need to make sure
you have on hand all the necessary ingredients and
utensils.

The servings noted at the close of the introductory
paragraph to each recipe are based on the following
formula: one serving is equal to 10 ounces—two 5-ounce
ladles or cups. The calorie information listed below the
servings is based on *Food Values of Portions Commonly
Used*, Church and Church, 12th edition revised, J. B.
Lippincott Company, 1975.

Many recipes, particularly those for soups that are
lighter and less robust than others, call for full-flavored
stock. That means the stock you use should be rich in
texture and taste. You can enrich your stock by adding,
in any combination, one or more of the ingredients listed
on page 28. Be sure to mix the stock well and taste it
after each new addition.

Many recipes call for pepper. Freshly ground pepper,
a noble spice for soups, is preferable but canned pepper
will do.

Most of the recipes call for salt. But you can make the
soups without it and not greatly affect the flavor. When
Consumers Union tested the recipes, all of the soups
were made without salt—it was served on the side. With

the taste for salt varying so widely you might wish to follow the same procedure and at the same time aid those who wish to cut down on salt intake.

A few recipes call for wine. If you wish, you can substitute fruit juice. For instance, if a recipe calls for 1 tablespoon of lemon juice plus wine, you can add 2 or 3 additional tablespoons of lemon juice in place of the wine. Or a half cup of apple juice in lieu of wine will do nicely.

Now a word or so about pots. When it comes to making soup—or stew, or anything requiring long cooking—there's nothing like a pot with good heat distribution. Ordinary lightweight aluminum or stainless steel pots tend to scorch in spots. Enamel-on-steel pots also tend to have poor heat distribution. A cast-iron pot would have to be extremely heavy to give the same heat distribution as a pot with a thick aluminum bottom. A good soup pot of about 4-quart size should have a tight-fitting cover and be made of heavy-gauge aluminum or of stainless steel with a thick aluminum bottom. You'll use it for the rest of your life.

Puréeing 2 or 3 cups of soup (with plenty of solids) and returning the purée to the pot makes the soup thicker. Many of the recipes call for this step; however, if you don't have a blender or food processor in which to make a purée, you can proceed without it. Or you can achieve some thickening by using a hand potato-masher.

Where a ladle is called for, a cup can be substituted.

Dilled chick-pea and chicken soup

If you absolutely can't get fresh dill—a plight common in some parts—you can substitute 2 teaspoons of dried dill, but be sure it's a fresh green color. If it's very dark it's likely to have lost most of its flavor.

SERVINGS: 6 to 8
CALORIES: About 290 if serving 6; 220 if serving 8

Place in a heavy 4-quart soup pot:

> *1 tablespoon cooking oil*
> *1 slice bacon, finely diced*

Heat until the bacon begins to sizzle. Add:

> *1 medium onion, peeled and finely chopped*
> *2 large stalks celery (including leaves), finely chopped*
> *2 large carrots, peeled and finely chopped*

Cook, covered, until the vegetables are moderately softened (about 15 minutes). Then add:

> *2 level tablespoons flour*
> *½ teaspoon ground sage*
> *1 bay leaf*
> *½ cup white wine*

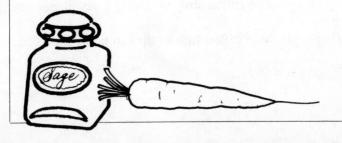

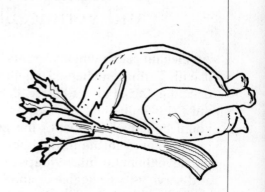

Bring to a simmer, uncovered. Cook for 10 minutes, stirring often. Remove the bay leaf. Add to the soup pot, mixing well:

3 cups chicken stock
2 cups water
1 teaspoon Worcestershire sauce

Place in the blender or food processor the entire contents of:

1 20-ounce can chick-peas

Purée well. Add the purée to the soup pot and bring to a good boil. Taste, and if necessary add:

salt
pepper

Mix into the soup:

1 cup cooked chicken, cut into thin strips
⅓ cup fresh dill, finely cut

Heat for a couple of minutes more.

Cream of leek and vermicelli soup

An elegant touch when you serve this soup is to dust it with Parmesan cheese (freshly grated, if possible), or add a dab of sweet butter. Because this soup uses only the bulb-ends and lower stems of the leeks, you'll be left with most of the green portions. They can be stored in the refrigerator in a jar with a tight lid. Save them for future soups or stews, or cook them and serve as a vegetable at another meal.

SERVINGS: 6 to 8
CALORIES: About 170 if serving 6; 130 if serving 8

Wash:

4 leeks

Cut the leeks down to 2 inches below where the green leaves separate from the whole stem. Slice the lower stems and bulbs lengthwise in half, then crosswise ¼-inch thick. Rinse thoroughly in cold water to remove any last bits of sand or grit; drain well. Melt in a heavy 4-quart soup pot:

3 tablespoons butter (or butter and margarine combined)

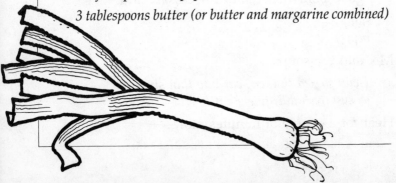

Sauté leeks gently, uncovered, in the melted butter over very low heat for about 15 minutes, stirring occasionally. Don't let them brown. Add:

2 level tablespoons flour

Mix well. Cook at very low heat for 10 minutes more, stirring now and then. Meanwhile, combine in a large saucepan:

4 cups chicken stock
1 teaspoon salt
¼ teaspoon ground white pepper

Bring to a boil, turn down the heat, and then ladle 1 cup of the seasoned chicken stock into the leek-and-flour mixture in the soup pot; mix well. Add to the soup pot:

2 cups milk

Cook the leek-flour-milk mixture gently, stirring often, for another 10 minutes. Turn off the heat. Now, bring the remaining 3 cups of chicken stock to a boil and add:

about 2 ounces vermicelli (or as many strands, held upright and pressed close together, as will cover a dime), broken up into small pieces a few inches long

Cook at a low boil, stirring often, for about 5 minutes, or until the vermicelli is as soft as you like it. Add the contents of the saucepan to the soup pot. Mix everything well, heating up if necessary.

Homey lima bean soup

You can add almost any herbs you like to this robust soup. Dried chervil is called for in the final step of cooking, but it is a delicate herb that loses its flavor if it has been on the shelf for a long time. So unless you have a fresh supply, consider using a substitute such as dried oregano or dried tarragon.

SERVINGS: 6 to 8
CALORIES: About 325 if serving 6; 240 if serving 8

Pour boiling water, to cover, over:

2 cups dried lima beans, large or small size

Let stand for 8 hours or so. (There will be very little water remaining.) After soaking the beans, put them—along with whatever water remains—in a heavy 4-quart soup pot. Add:

6 cups chicken stock

Bring to a good simmer. Lower the heat, cover, and cook at a low simmer for about 1 hour and 30 minutes, until the lima beans are quite soft. Meanwhile, sauté in a covered saucepan:

3 tablespoons butter
2 medium onions, peeled and chopped
2 medium carrots, peeled and sliced into thin rounds

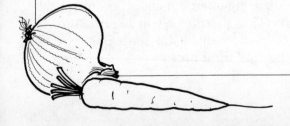

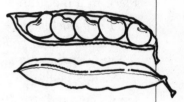

Cook until the onions and carrots are soft but not browned. Lift the cover now and then to mix. Add the vegetables to the soup pot any time during the first hour. (After having cooked for about 1 hour and 30 minutes, the lima beans should be quite soft.) Taste to see if you need to add:

> salt

Pour 2 cups of the soup (including plenty of solids) into the blender or food processor and purée. Return the purée to the soup pot. Pulverize between the palms of your hands and sprinkle onto the soup:

> *1 teaspoon dried chervil*

Stir and bring the soup to a good simmer.

Chilled green pea and cucumber bisque

As delightful as a summer's day. And as easy to prepare as it is delicious to eat. Make it in the cool of the morning and serve it chilled in the heat of the afternoon.

SERVINGS: 6 to 8
CALORIES: About 310 if serving 6; 235 if serving 8

Place in a medium-sized saucepan:

1 cup chicken stock
1 small onion, peeled and chopped
½ teaspoon ground cumin or curry powder
½ teaspoon salt

Cook, covered, for 10 minutes at a good simmer. Put contents into the blender or food processor and when the mixture is thoroughly puréed, pour into a 5- to 6-quart bowl. Then, using the same saucepan, bring to a boil:

1 additional cup chicken stock
4 cups fresh green peas or 2 10-ounce packages thawed
*   frozen green peas*

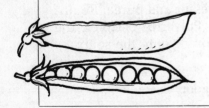

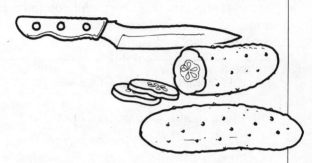

Cook at a low boil, uncovered, stirring occasionally. Cook 6 minutes for fresh peas, 3 minutes for frozen peas. Place the cooked peas in the blender or food processor, purée, and add to the soup bowl. Then put into the blender or food processor:

1 cup water
2 large cucumbers, peeled, seeded, and diced

Purée thoroughly and add to the soup bowl. Lastly, add to the soup bowl:

1 additional cup chicken stock
1 cup heavy cream
1 cup sour cream
juice of ½ lemon, strained

Mix well with a whisk, then chill for at least 4 hours. Before serving, sprinkle on each bowl:

finely chopped chives.

Parsnip soup

The parsnip, very sweet when cooked, is an unde-
servedly neglected vegetable. If you think you don't
like parsnips, try this soup, and you may change your
mind. It not only tastes good, but its aroma is particularly fresh and delightful.

SERVINGS: 6 to 8
CALORIES: About 165 if serving 6; 120 if serving 8

Place in a heavy 4-quart soup pot:

4 tablespoons butter (or margarine)
1 pound parsnips, peeled and quartered, and sliced or
coarsely chopped
1 cup celery (including leaves), chopped

Sauté, stirring with a wooden spoon until the vegetables are coated with butter. Cover and continue to
cook over medium heat for 10 minutes, stirring occasionally. Meanwhile, heat in a saucepan:

3 cups chicken stock

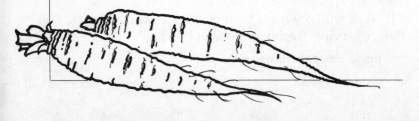

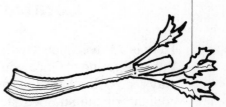

When the parsnip-celery mixture has cooked for the prescribed 10 minutes, add the stock to the soup pot. Stir well, then put 1 cup of the soup (containing plenty of solids) into the blender or food processor along with:

> *3 level tablespoons flour*
> *1 cup cold water*
> *¼ teaspoon grated nutmeg*
> *1 teaspoon salt*

Blend at high speed until everything is well puréed. Pour the purée into the soup pot. Add:

> *2 cups water*

Heat, uncovered, to a good simmer for 5 minutes, stirring occasionally. Season to taste with:

> *pepper*

Pour into the blender another cup of soup with plenty of solids and add:

> *⅓ cup parsley, chopped*

Blend well and add the purée to the soup pot and heat to a good simmer. Before serving sprinkle on each bowl of soup:

> *grated Parmesan cheese (freshly grated, if possible).*

Caraway soup

Here is a velvety soup with a delicate caraway flavor. But one caution: Once you've strained out the caraway seeds, don't boil the soup for too long. Too much cooking of the strained stock will reduce the flavor of the caraway. Pepper enhances this soup, so invite those who like that seasoning to use a pepper mill at the table.

SERVINGS: 6 to 8
CALORIES: About 170 if serving 6; 125 if serving 8

Add to a heavy 4-quart soup pot:

7 cups full-flavored chicken stock (see page 28)
3 tablespoons caraway seeds

Stir well, bring to a boil, then lower the heat, cover, and keep at a low simmer for about 20 minutes. Strain, discard the caraway seeds, and return the stock to the soup pot, keeping it on low heat. In a medium-sized skillet, melt:

7 tablespoons butter (or butter and margarine combined)

Reduce the heat to very, very low and mix in a little at a time:

7 level tablespoons flour

Keep mixing the flour and butter (use a whisk to avoid lumps) until the mixture is completely smooth and the flour is thoroughly worked in. Turn off the heat. Add a ladleful of the hot stock to the flour and butter, combining carefully until the mixture is smooth. Do the same with another ladleful of stock, following the same procedure until the flour-butter-stock mixture is well thinned. It can then be added to the rest of the stock in the soup pot. Stir the soup mixture strenuously with the whisk, then heat the soup slowly to a full boil. Turn off the heat immediately and pour a bit of soup into a cup and taste for seasoning. Seasoning will depend on how the original stock was seasoned. You may want to add:

salt
pepper

Stir again before ladling into bowls. Sprinkle over each bowl:

finely chopped hard-boiled egg
a couple of sprigs of fresh parsley or dill.

Vegetable soup

This hearty soup is delicious. It's more delicious if made in the morning and left on the stove, covered, for a few hours. It's most delicious the second day. And it makes a good beginning for a continuing soup pot if you keep adding leftover vegetables and the liquid that the vegetables have been cooked in. After each such addition, heat the soup just to boiling before serving.

SERVINGS: 6 to 8
CALORIES: About 165 if serving 6; 125 if serving 8

First, cut the following vegetables into small pieces:

   1 *large green pepper, seeded*
   2 *medium-to-large onions, peeled*
   2 *medium tomatoes*
   3 *large garlic cloves, peeled*
   2 *medium potatoes, peeled or unpeeled*
   3 *large carrots, peeled or unpeeled*
   3 *or more stalks celery (including leaves)*

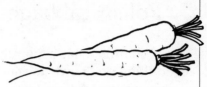

Then in a heavy 4-quart soup pot heat until bubbling:

4 teaspoons cooking oil
1 tablespoon butter (or margarine)

Add the prepared vegetables to the soup pot and mix with a wooden spoon until the vegetables are lightly coated with the oil mixture. Don't let the heat get too high—keep everything at a gentle sauté. Cook, uncovered, for about 10 minutes, mixing now and then. Add the following stock and seasoning:

3 cups chicken or meat stock
3 cups water
2 teaspoons fresh, or 1 teaspoon dried, basil or dill
1 tablespoon Worcestershire sauce
¼ teaspoon pepper

Cover the pot and cook very slowly, at a bare simmer, for about 1 hour and 30 minutes. Stir occasionally. After the soup has simmered for about 1 hour and 30 minutes, dip out 4 cups of the soup with plenty of the vegetables and pour into the blender or food processor. Purée until smooth and put back into the soup pot. Add:

½ cup elbow macaroni, uncooked

Stir well. Cover the pot and cook very slowly for another 30 minutes or so, stirring occasionally.

Polish cabbage-potato soup

Great country fare: a potful brimming with almost everything one needs to stay alive and keep healthy. Another soup that improves unbelievably with age (even as you and I do). Make plenty so there'll be some left for the second or third day.

SERVINGS: 6 to 8
CALORIES: About 435 if serving 6; 325 if serving 8

Cook at a simmer, covered, for about 1 hour:

> *3 cups water*
> *1 cup dried yellow split peas*

Continue cooking until the peas are very soft, almost like a porridge (or soak the split peas in the water for 8 hours or more and then cook for 15 to 20 minutes). While the peas are cooking, place in a heavy 4-quart soup pot:

> *2 cups water*
> *2 fairly large potatoes, peeled and diced*
> *1 tablespoon butter (or margarine)*

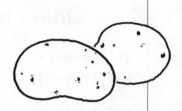

Cook at a high simmer, covered, until the potatoes are almost soft (15 to 20 minutes). While the potatoes are cooking, place in a fairly large unheated skillet:

2 slices bacon, diced
1 large onion, peeled and diced

Cook over medium heat, stirring often, until all the fat has been rendered from the bacon and the diced onion is soft. With a slotted spoon, remove the cooked potatoes from their liquid and set aside. Add to the potato water:

4 cups chicken or meat stock
½ pound cabbage (about half a small head), cut into small pieces
¼ teaspoon pepper

Bring to a high simmer. Cover and cook for about 10 minutes. Put the potatoes back into the soup pot along with the cooked split peas and the bacon-onion mixture. Then add:

1 1-pound can sauerkraut (including liquid)
1 or 2 cups any leftover meat, sausage, etc., cut into pieces

Mix well. Before serving, heat for 5 minutes after the pot reaches bubbling.

Onion mushroom soup

This recipe asks you to peel an entire head of garlic cloves and to grate a half cup of Swiss cheese. Don't fret. To prepare the garlic: Separate the cloves, cover with boiling water, let stand for 30 seconds, strain, and cover with cold water for a few seconds. They'll practically peel themselves. For the Swiss cheese: Cut into very small cubes and toss them into the blender or food processor, and run at high speed.

SERVINGS: 6 to 8
CALORIES: About 170 if serving 6; 130 if serving 8

Sauté in a heavy 4-quart soup pot:

> *1 tablespoon cooking oil*
> *2 tablespoons butter (or margarine)*
> *1½ pounds onions, peeled and chopped*

Cook until the onions are lightly browned. Then add:

> *4 cups chicken or meat stock*
> *2 cups water*
> *1 large head of garlic cloves, separated and peeled*

Bring to a simmer, then cover and cook slowly for about 30 minutes. Meanwhile, in a skillet sauté:

1 tablespoon butter
½ pound mushrooms, caps and stems, sliced thin

(You will find that 1 tablespoon of butter is enough. The mushrooms will shortly release their own liquid to help in their cooking.) After the mushrooms have entirely absorbed the butter and have become soft but not dry, remove the pan from the heat. Strain the onions and garlic from the stock with a slotted spoon and run them in the blender or food processor until they're uniformly puréed. Put the purée back into the soup pot. Mix, taste, and if necessary add:

salt
pepper

Put the sautéed mushrooms into the soup pot and simmer, covered, for another 10 minutes. Have ready to sprinkle over the bowls of soup before serving:

½ cup grated Swiss cheese.

Thick golden curried potato soup

Now here's a soup that will really put meat on your bones! But it may also cause some controversy. When it comes to curry, people have markedly different tastes. Some like their curry hot, others prefer it mild. The strength of curry powders differs, too. Use the moderate amount this recipe calls for, then taste the soup before serving. You can always add more, but then bring the soup to a slow boil before serving. Remember to stir this soup often to keep the split peas from settling to the bottom and scorching.

SERVINGS: 6 to 8
CALORIES: About 230 if serving 6; 175 if serving 8

Bring to a boil in a heavy 4-quart soup pot:

3 cups water
1 cup dried yellow split peas

Then turn the heat down to a simmer and cook for 10 minutes. Next, add to the soup pot:

1 cup water
1 pound carrots, peeled and sliced in thin rounds

Bring the pot to a boil once again. Turn down to a simmer and cook, covered, for another 30 minutes or so until the carrots and the split peas are quite soft. Stir the contents often. While the pot is simmering, place in a medium-sized skillet:

2 tablespoons butter
1 large onion, peeled and chopped

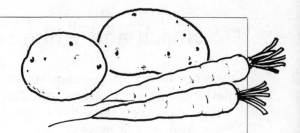

Cook slowly until the onion is very soft (about 20 minutes). In a small pot, cook until moderately soft but not mushy (about 15 minutes):

   1 cup water
   2 medium potatoes, peeled and diced
   1 teaspoon salt

Drain the carrots and split peas from the cooking water, reserving the latter. Add the onion in its butter to the vegetables and place the mixture in the blender or food processor and run until you have a uniform purée. Pour this back into the soup pot with the liquid. Now, add to the soup pot:

   2 cups full-flavored chicken or meat stock (see page 28)
   ½ teaspoon curry powder
   ½ teaspoon powdered garlic
   1 tablespoon honey

Mix well with a whisk. Then, while you bring the soup pot to a good simmer, drain the potatoes and add their cooking liquid to the soup pot. When the soup pot reaches a simmer, add the cooked diced potatoes, mix all gently but well, and bring again to a simmer. You might want to add just before serving:

   pepper.

Spinach and white bean soup

Another hearty soup—unusual, with a rich spinach flavor mixed with carrots and beans. You can't go wrong when you serve this soup—but be warned, it takes four pots to make it.

SERVINGS: 6 to 8
CALORIES: About 240 if serving 6; 180 if serving 8

Bring to a boil in a covered saucepan:

> 2½ cups water
> ¾ cup dried white pea beans or navy beans

Then lower to a simmer and cook for about 1 hour and 15 minutes. Place in another saucepan:

> 1 cup boiling water
> 4 peeled carrots, sliced into very thin rounds (old or large carrots should be cut in half lengthwise before you slice them)

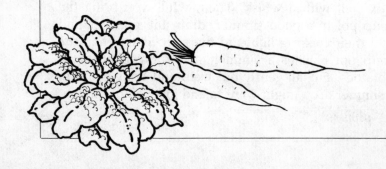

Cook carrots, covered, at moderate heat for about 10 minutes or until tender. Heat in a third saucepan:

1 cup boiling water
1 10-ounce package frozen chopped spinach

Break the spinach up with a fork until completely thawed. Bring to a boil and then turn off the heat and let the spinach stand. Put in a heavy 4-quart soup pot:

1 tablespoon cooking oil
½ pound lean ground beef

Heat slowly, stirring, until the meat begins to sizzle. Then add:

4 medium-to-large garlic cloves, sliced
1 fairly large onion, peeled and chopped
¼ teaspoon caraway seeds

Cook slowly, stirring, until the meat is no longer pink. Put the ground beef mixture and the cooked spinach, with all their liquids, in the blender or food processor and finely purée. Pour the purée into the soup pot. Drain the carrots, put their cooking liquid into the soup pot, and set the carrots aside. Next, add to the soup pot:

2 cups chicken or meat stock
1 tablespoon soy sauce
1 teaspoon salt
¼ teaspoon pepper

Heat, stirring, until the soup simmers smartly. Add the cooked beans and cook for 5 minutes. Add the carrot slices and heat for another minute.

Garden bounty soup

As its name implies, this soup is bursting with nour-ishment. It looks it too.

SERVINGS: 6 to 8
CALORIES: About 180 if serving 6; 135 if serving 8

Heat until bubbling in a heavy 4-quart soup pot:

   2 tablespoons cooking oil

Add:

   1 medium onion, peeled and chopped
   2 medium tomatoes, chopped
   15 or so raw string beans, diced

Cook lightly, stirring occasionally, until the onion becomes translucent. Add to the soup pot and mix well:

   1 small-to-medium eggplant, peeled and diced

Cover and cook over low heat for 5 minutes, stirring now and then. Add:

   6 cups chicken or meat stock

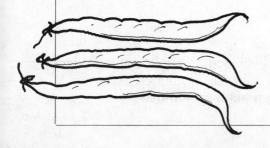

Bring the pot to a near boil. Then turn down the heat, cover, and simmer for about 20 minutes. Strain into a saucepan 2 cups of liquid from the soup pot, and into this put:

2 cups fresh, or 1 10-ounce package frozen, lima beans

Cook until tender, about 15 minutes. Then pour the beans and cooking water into the blender or food processor and purée until smooth. Mix the purée into the soup pot. Add and mix well:

1 tablespoon prepared mustard (preferably Dijon or Pommery)

Heat and taste for seasoning. Add, if desired:

salt
pepper

Bring the soup to a boil.

Asparagus and tomato minestrone

To make this delicate yet quite filling soup, there's no need to buy the most expensive of the canned asparagus. Buy the can that costs the least—usually the type that contains cut pieces of green asparagus, which makes the blending easier.

SERVINGS: 6 to 8
CALORIES: About 225 if serving 6; 170 if serving 8

Put into a heavy 4-quart soup pot:

> 3 tablespoons butter (or margarine)
> 2 medium tomatoes, diced

Cook rapidly over high heat until tomatoes become slightly soft. Meanwhile, in a saucepan, boil:

> 2 cups water

Then add to the boiling water:

> ¼ pound uncooked spaghetti, broken into 2-inch lengths

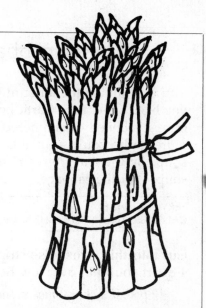

Cook, stirring now and then, until the spaghetti is as soft as you like it. Add to the soup pot. Then put into the blender or food processor:

1 14½-ounce can cut asparagus (including liquid)
¼ teaspoon ground nutmeg
½ teaspoon salt
¼ teaspoon pepper

Blend thoroughly. Add the purée to the soup pot along with:

3 cups chicken or meat stock

Heat the soup to a good simmer. Add:

½ cup heavy cream

Stir well and let cook at a simmer for 5 minutes before serving.

Green cabbage soup

You can double the amount of garlic in this soup, if you like. Never fear: Garlic becomes sweet and gentle once it's boiled or simmered for a long time. So the more garlic you use in this recipe, the sweeter the soup. By the way, "green" refers to the color of the soup—not the cabbage.

SERVINGS: 6 to 8
CALORIES: About 170 if serving 6; 130 if serving 8

Cut into thin, crosswise strips and place in a heavy 4-quart soup pot over low heat:

¼ pound hickory-smoked bacon

When the bacon begins to sizzle slightly, add:

2 stalks celery (including leaves), sliced thin, crosswise
2 carrots, peeled and sliced into thin rounds
½ small head of cabbage, cut into chunks, then sliced thin
2 or more garlic cloves, peeled and sliced

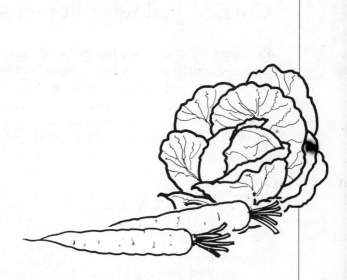

Cook, uncovered, over a low flame for about 20 minutes. Stir now and then with a wooden spoon. Then add:

4 cups chicken or meat stock
4 cups water
½ teaspoon salt

Simmer, covered, over very low heat for about 1 hour, stirring occasionally. Meanwhile, thaw:

1 10-ounce package frozen chopped spinach

Drain the spinach, adding its liquid to the soup pot. Place the spinach in the blender or food processor. Add to the spinach 1 cup of the soup (solids included) and purée. Pour the purée into the soup pot and stir. Bring to a boil before serving.

Curried yellow split pea soup

This robust soup calls for nutmeg and curry. See the remarks on curry powder in the introduction to thick golden curried potato soup, page 66. And remember that any soup containing split peas has to be stirred a bit more often than most soups in order to keep the split peas from settling to the bottom and possibly scorching.

SERVINGS: 6 to 8
CALORIES: About 260 if serving 6; 195 if serving 8

Cook in a heavy 4-quart soup pot:

> *3 cups water*
> *2 cups dried yellow split peas*

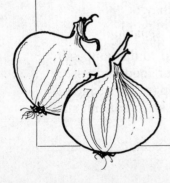

The peas should cook at a simmer, covered, until they are fairly soft (about 1 hour). Stir occasionally to keep the peas from sticking. When they are done, put 1 cup (2, if you like a thicker soup) into the blender or food processor and purée. Pour the purée back into the soup pot and add:

6 cups chicken or meat stock
2 small onions, peeled and sliced into very thin rings
½ teaspoon curry powder
¼ teaspoon grated nutmeg
1 teaspoon salt
pepper

Bring to a near boil. Turn the heat down and cook, covered, for about 20 minutes, stirring occasionally.

Overland gumbo

This soup has a Creole soul. All of its ingredients—from corn to okra—make it thick and delicious. Before you prepare it, check comments on curry powder in the introduction to thick golden curried potato soup on page 66.

SERVINGS: 6 to 8
CALORIES: About 230 if serving 6; 170 if serving 8

Melt in a heavy 4-quart soup pot:

3 tablespoons butter (or margarine)

When the butter just begins to sizzle, add:

2 medium onions, peeled and cut into eighths
1 medium green pepper, cut into strips
¼ teaspoon curry powder

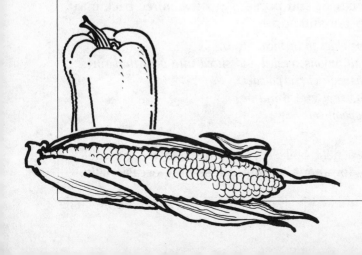

Mix well. Cover, keep the heat low, and stir occasionally. Cook until the onions and green pepper are soft but not browned. Add:

1⅓ cups cooked lean ham, diced

Increase the heat. Cook, uncovered, stirring often, for 5 minutes. Add:

2 cups chicken or meat stock
1 1-pound can tomatoes (including liquid)
1 1-pound can cream-style corn
½ teaspoon celery seed

Bring the pot to a good simmer. Add:

1 10-ounce package frozen sliced okra

Stir the contents of the soup pot until the okra is thawed. When the pot again reaches a simmer, cover, and cook for another 10 minutes.

Zucchini soup

A tasty soup, this, though not a thick one. You know, of course, that you can thicken almost any soup by puréeing 1 or 2 cups of the soup with plenty of its solids and mixing the purée back into the soup. This particular soup is also delicious entirely puréed and served hot, hot, hot.

SERVINGS: 6 to 8
CALORIES: About 135 if serving 6; 100 if serving 8

Heat in a heavy 4-quart soup pot:

>   *2 tablespoons cooking oil*

Add:

>   *1 cup onion, peeled and diced*

Cook, uncovered, until the onion is translucent. Add to the soup pot:

>   3 *level tablespoons cornstarch, mixed with 1 cup water*
>   2 *medium-to-large zucchini, scrubbed, quartered lengthwise, and sliced*
>   5 *cups full-flavored chicken or meat stock (see page 28)*

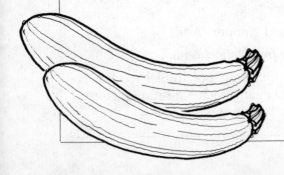

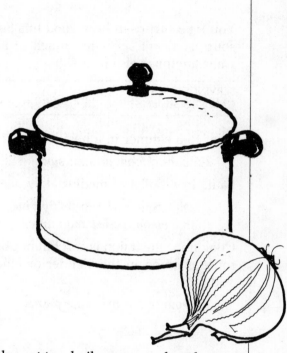

Mix well. Bring the pot to a boil, cover, and cook over medium-low heat for about 15 minutes. Then add:

> 1 4-ounce jar pimientos, diced (including liquid)

Mix well. Then add:

> 1 teaspoon dried basil
> ¼ cup grated Parmesan cheese (freshly grated, if possible)
> salt
> pepper.

Peanut butter soup

You'll be surprised how good this Southern-inspired soup is. Don't serve too much of it or no one will want anything else to eat.

SERVINGS: 6 to 8
CALORIES: About 395 if serving 6; 295 if serving 8

Heat to a simmer in a heavy 4-quart soup pot:

> *2½ cups chicken or meat stock*

Sauté in a skillet at medium-low heat:

> *2 tablespoons butter (or margarine)*
> *1 large onion, peeled and minced*

Cook until the onion is soft but not browned. Put the sautéed onion in the blender or food processor and add:

> *1 20-ounce can red kidney beans*

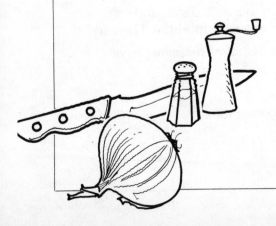

Purée the contents of the can of beans with the onion. (You may need to add a little of the heated stock to aid in blending.) Add the purée to the soup pot. Then combine in the blender or food processor:

1 additional cup chicken or meat stock
1 8-ounce jar (1 cup) peanut butter, preferably smooth

Blend until uniformly puréed. Add the purée to the soup pot. Mix well with a whisk. Heat the contents of the pot slowly, stirring all the while so that the soup at the bottom of the pot won't burn. As soon as the soup is hot but not boiling, remove from the heat. Taste for seasoning and if necessary add:

salt
pepper

Have ready to sprinkle over the bowls of soup before serving:

a few strips of well-cooked bacon, blotted and crumbled.

Brown potato soup

Here's a real old-world "Mom's" soup, thick and filling. Notice what a good touch the cinnamon gives it. (Don't tell your guests about the cinnamon; see if they can guess.)

SERVINGS: 6 to 8
CALORIES: About 145 if serving 6; 108 if serving 8

Sauté in a heavy 4-quart soup pot:

> 1 tablespoon butter (or margarine)
> 1 good-sized onion, peeled and diced
> ½ cup celery (including leaves), diced

Stir often over medium-high heat. Cook until the vegetables become quite soft and begin to brown slightly (about 15 minutes). Add to the soup pot:

> 1 tablespoon butter (or margarine)
> 4 or 5 medium potatoes, peeled and diced
> 1 teaspoon salt
> ¼ teaspoon pepper

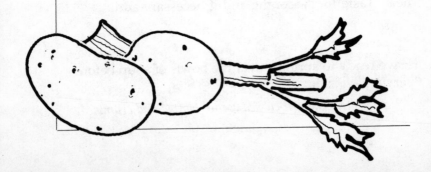

Turn the heat down to medium. Cook, uncovered, stirring often and scraping the bottom (a wooden spoon is best for this) until the potatoes begin to brown slightly. Add, stirring until melted:

1 tablespoon butter (or margarine)

Then add:

2 level tablespoons flour

Heat until the flour begins to brown and then add:

½ teaspoon cinnamon

Mix all very well. Heat in a saucepan:

5 cups full-flavored chicken or meat stock (see page 28)

Add the stock, a cup at a time, to the soup pot, stirring thoroughly each time until the flour has been well integrated into the liquid. After adding the last of the stock, bring the pot to a boil and lower the heat to medium-low. Cook, covered, for about 20 minutes, stirring occasionally. Pour 1 cup of the soup, containing plenty of solids, into the blender or food processor; blend thoroughly. Return the purée to the soup pot. Add:

3 tablespoons parsley, finely chopped

Bring the soup to steaming.

Cream of cauliflower and cheese soup

Here's a good rich soup: fine anytime, but really soul-warming on a cold winter's day. If you don't have basil you can substitute finely chopped fresh parsley (or summer savory, if you can find a jar of it). When preparing this soup you will find you are left with the cauliflower stalks. The small tender ones can be diced and cooked, then puréed and added to the soup if you want it thicker. The larger stalks can be saved, diced, cooked, and served as a vegetable at another meal.

SERVINGS: 6 to 8
CALORIES: About 195 if serving 6; 145 if serving 8

Into a heavy 4-quart soup pot put:

   3 cups water
   1 medium onion, peeled and finely chopped
   2 teaspoons dried basil
   1 teaspoon salt
   ¼ teaspoon pepper

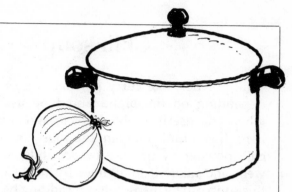

Cook, covered, for 5 minutes over medium heat. Add:

> *2½ to 3 cups cauliflower flowerets, cut to uniform size,*
> *from a medium-sized head*

Continue to cook, covered, until the cauliflower is soft, about 15 minutes. In a medium-sized saucepan combine:

> *2 tablespoons melted butter (or margarine)*
> *2 level tablespoons flour*

Mix until none of the flour remains white. Then slowly add to the butter and flour mixture:

> *1 cup hot chicken or meat stock*

Stir with a whisk until the mixture is smooth. Pour into the soup pot and mix well. Heat in a saucepan:

> *2 cups milk*

Then add to the milk:

> *¼ pound cheddar cheese, cut into small pieces*

Cook the mixture over low heat, stirring until all the cheese is melted. Add to the soup pot. Mix well and heat until the soup begins to steam.

Chili soup

Chili powder, like curry powder, varies in strength depending on the brand and type used. Go easy when you use it. Only a half teaspoon is called for here. If you find you want the soup hotter, add more chili powder by quarter-teaspoonfuls, stir the soup well, and allow it to simmer further. Good as it is, this soup can be made better by adding bits of leftover meat.

SERVINGS: 6 to 8
CALORIES: About 210 if serving 6; 160 if serving 8

Heat in a heavy 4-quart soup pot:

> 2 *tablespoons cooking oil*

Add to the oil:

> 2 *medium onions, peeled and chopped*
> 1 *large stalk celery (including leaves), diced*
> 4 or 5 *medium tomatoes, sliced*
> ½ *teaspoon ground cumin*
> ½ *teaspoon chili powder*
> 1 *teaspoon salt*

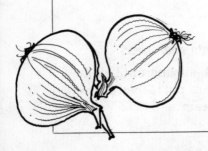

Stir well. Cover and cook for 10 minutes over medium heat, stirring occasionally. Add and bring to a low boil:

4 cups full-flavored meat stock (see page 28)

Add:

¾ cup elbow macaroni, uncooked

Cover and continue to cook, stirring now and then to prevent the macaroni from sticking to the bottom. When the macaroni is as soft as you like it, add:

1 1-pound can red kidney beans (pink kidney beans can be substituted, if necessary)

Mix well. Pour 1 cup of the soup (be sure it has plenty of solids in it) into the blender or food processor and purée. Pour the purée back into the soup. Taste the soup to see if more chili powder is needed, and mix well.

Sausage soup

Here's a one-dish meal. Serve it with chunks of crusty bread and you'll need nothing else.

SERVINGS: 6 to 8
CALORIES: About 255 if serving 6; 195 if serving 8

Put into a heavy 4-quart soup pot:

> *½ pound sausage (spiced or mild), cut into small pieces*

Cook slowly over low heat, stirring, until the meat gives up its fat and begins to curl. If less than 1 tablespoon of fat is produced, add enough cooking oil to bring it to this amount. If more than this is rendered, remove and discard all but a tablespoon of it. Add to the soup pot:

> *1 medium onion, peeled and chopped*
> *1 whole clove*
> *2 stalks celery (including leaves), chopped*
> *½ medium head of cabbage, finely shredded*
> *3 good-sized potatoes, peeled and diced*
> *½ cup scallion greens or chives, snipped into small pieces*
> *½ teaspoon dried oregano, well rubbed between the palms*

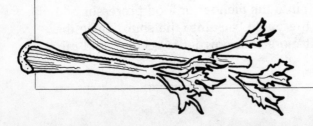

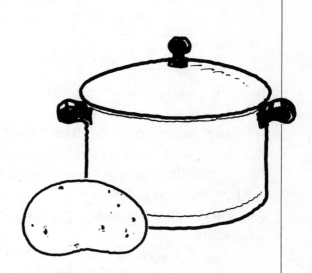

Heat slowly. Stir until the vegetables are a little softened. Add:

5 cups meat stock
3 cups water

Bring to a near boil. Turn the heat down, cover, and
simmer for about 1 hour. Add:

salt
pepper

Stir well before serving.

Sweet and sour cabbage soup

Here's a real country soup—and like some of life's other blessings, it's good the second or third time around. The recipe calls for 1 pound of cabbage: that's 5 firmly packed cups of shredded cabbage.

SERVINGS: 6 to 8
CALORIES: About 380 if serving 6; 285 if serving 8

Sauté in a heavy 4-quart soup pot:

3 tablespoons butter (or margarine)
3 large onions, peeled and chopped small

Stir occasionally, cooking until the onions are translucent. Into the soup pot drain only the liquid from:

1 28-ounce can peeled tomatoes

Chop the canned tomatoes and add them to the pot. Also add:

3 cups meat stock
½ cup brown sugar
4 whole cloves
juice of 1 lemon, unstrained but with pits removed
1 teaspoon salt

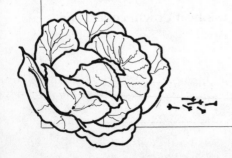

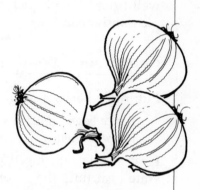

Bring the soup pot to a boil. Stir, turn down the heat, cover, and simmer for about 30 minutes. Put into the blender or food processor:

> 1 20-ounce can chick-peas or white kidney beans (can-nellini)

Purée the contents of the canned peas or beans until smooth and then add the purée to the soup pot. Mix very well. Add to the soup pot:

> 1 pound cabbage, shredded

Mix well. Raise the heat very slightly. Simmer for about 15 minutes more. The cabbage should be slightly crisp at the end of cooking.

Fish chowder

Here's a soup that really should be made with fresh fish. You can use any variety, fresh water or salt. If you live where you can't get fresh fish and must use frozen, be sure it's of good quality and has been kept well frozen. Don't pick any package that smells unpleasantly fishy.

SERVINGS: 6 to 8
CALORIES: About 355 if serving 6; 265 if serving 8

Put into a heavy 4-quart soup pot:

1 slice bacon, diced small
1 medium onion, peeled, quartered, and sliced

Heat slowly, stirring. Continue cooking over moderate heat until the onion is translucent. Add to the soup pot:

4 cups fish stock
3 good-sized potatoes, peeled and diced
2 stalks celery (including leaves), diced
a few sprigs of fresh parsley
¼ teaspoon pepper

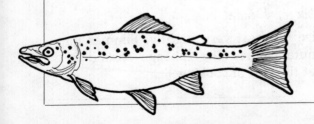

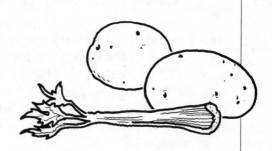

Heat until the contents send up steam. Cover and keep at a simmer for about 20 minutes, until the potatoes are tender. (They shouldn't become too soft.) Turn off the heat and keep covered. In a saucepan, heat:

> *2 cups milk*
> *4 tablespoons butter (or margarine)*

When this mixture is very warm, put it into the blender or food processor with:

> *6 level tablespoons flour*

Blend until well mixed. Pour the purée into the soup pot, mix well, and add:

> *1 pound boneless fish of any kind (fresh, if possible; but if frozen, thaw first), diced to about the same size as the diced potatoes*

Heat for 5 minutes, keeping the pot below a boil. Cook only until the fish is cooked through, no longer than 3 minutes. Taste and add, if necessary:

> *salt.*

Emerald isle fish soup

This beautifully green tasty soup can be made thicker by puréeing in the blender or food processor several pieces of the potatoes that have cooked in the soup, and then mixing the purée well into the soup. Like most soups, this one is first-rate when reheated. But the soup won't stay as bright a green as when it was first made.

SERVINGS: 6 to 8
CALORIES: About 185 if serving 6; 140 if serving 8

Thaw, drain if necessary, and set aside, uncooked:

2 10-ounce packages frozen peas

Into a heavy 4-quart soup pot put:

4 cups fish stock
4 cups water
4 medium potatoes, peeled and diced large
2 large carrots, peeled and cut into thick rounds
2 large onions, peeled and cut into eighths

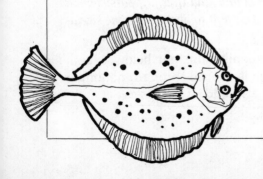

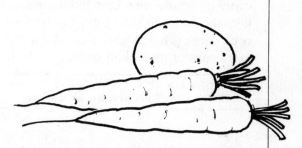

Bring to a boil and then lower to a simmer and cook, covered, for about 1 hour. Place in a small skillet:

> 1 *tablespoon olive oil*
> 2 *large garlic cloves, peeled and finely diced*

Heat oil and garlic until the garlic just begins to crisp (don't let it brown). Add the contents of the skillet to the soup pot along with:

> 1 *pound fish fillets of any kind (fresh, if possible; but*
> *if frozen, thaw first), cut into strips or chunks*
> ½ *teaspoon poultry seasoning or dried sage*
> ½ *cup parsley, coarsely chopped*
> 1 *teaspoonful salt*
> *pepper*

Simmer the mixture for another 5 minutes. Put the thawed, drained peas into the blender or food processor with about 2 cups of the soup liquid and purée. Add the purée to the soup. Mix well and simmer for another 5 minutes.

Clam and corn chowder

A real Yankee soup. Instead of raw corn you can use canned, whole corn kernels (drained), or frozen corn kernels, but you won't get the flavor that fresh corn cobs give. (This is also a good way to use up a few extra ears of uncooked corn.)

SERVINGS: 6 to 8
CALORIES: About 320 if serving 6; 240 if serving 8

Strip:

3 ears corn, uncooked

Stand an ear of corn on end on a cutting board, and with a sharp knife cut down close to the cob; turn and repeat until all the kernels are removed. Place the kernels in a medium-sized skillet and set aside. Break the cobs in half and put them into a heavy 4-quart soup pot with:

2 cups water
2 medium potatoes, peeled and diced

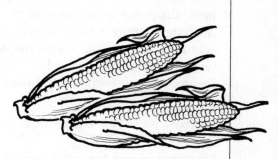

Bring to a low boil. Cook, covered, for 10 minutes. Remove the corn cobs and discard them. Add to the skillet containing the corn kernels:

2 tablespoons butter (or margarine)
1 small onion, peeled and finely chopped

Sauté, stirring frequently, until the onion and corn have become quite dry and have begun to brown slightly. Add these to the soup pot along with:

2 cups fish stock
1 cup milk
1 cup heavy cream
2 6½-ounce cans minced clams, including liquid
1 teaspoon salt
pepper

Mix well. Then put 2 cups (containing plenty of solids) into the blender or food processor and purée. Pour the purée back into the soup pot, heat to a good simmer—don't boil—and serve.

Italian red fish soup

This recipe calls for fresh ripe peeled tomatoes. To peel, drop the tomatoes into boiling water and immediately remove the pot from the heat and let it stand for 15 seconds. Pierce the skin of the tomatoes with the tip of the paring knife and peel away. Serve this lusty soup with crusty bread.

SERVINGS: 6 to 8
CALORIES: About 200 if serving 6; 150 if serving 8

Heat in a heavy 4-quart soup pot:

> 2 *tablespoons olive oil*
> 2 *tablespoons cooking oil*

Add and cook until brown:

> 1 *garlic clove, sliced lengthwise*

With a slotted spoon or a fork remove and discard the browned garlic and let the oil cool somewhat. Then add to the oil:

> 1 *garlic clove, peeled and finely chopped*
> ½ *cup parsley (Italian parsley, if possible), finely chopped*
> 1 *teaspoon dried basil, well rubbed between the palms*

Stir and cook over low heat for about 2 minutes. Then add:

> 3 or 4 *medium fresh tomatoes, peeled and coarsely chopped*

Raise the heat to moderate. Cover and cook for 10 minutes, stirring occasionally. Now add:

> 4 *cups fish stock*
> 2 *cups water*
> 1 *pound fish fillets of any kind (fresh, if possible; but if frozen, thaw first), cut into small pieces*
> *juice of 1 lemon, pits removed*
> ¼ *teaspoon pepper*

Cook, covered, for 10 minutes more. Taste to see if you need to add:

> *salt.*

Land and sea fish chowder

The recipe calls for crackers: oyster or regular. If you use saltines, be sure to use less salt in the preparation of the chowder. For a note on dried versus fresh dill, see the introduction to creamy salmon soup, page 104.

SERVINGS: 6 to 8
CALORIES: About 305 if serving 6; 235 if serving 8

Put into a heavy 4-quart soup pot:

> 1 cup water
> 3 medium potatoes, peeled and diced
> 2 medium carrots, peeled and sliced
> 1 large stalk celery (including leaves), diced
> 1 small onion, peeled and sliced

Heat to a steady simmer, then cook very slowly, covered, until the carrots are fairly soft (about 15 minutes). Add to the soup pot:

> 2 cups fish stock
> 1 pound boneless fish of any kind (fresh, if possible; but if frozen, thaw first), cut into chunks

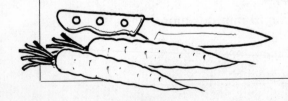

Again heat to a simmer, mix well, cover, and cook for 5 minutes. Then add:

⅓ cup fresh dill, finely cut, or 1 tablespoon dried dill
2 cups milk
1 cup light cream
1 teaspoon salt
¼ teaspoon pepper

When the mixture reaches a simmer once more, taste to see if more salt and pepper are needed. Before ladling the chowder, have ready to put into each bowl:

oyster crackers or regular crackers, crushed

Lightly sprinkle on each bowl of chowder:

paprika.

Creamy salmon chowder

This is a pink, delicious, heartwarming soup. If you use dried instead of fresh dill, see that it's bright green, otherwise the dill won't have much flavor and you'll lose that special touch of color.

SERVINGS: 6 to 8
CALORIES: About 450 if serving 6; 340 if serving 8

Bring to a boil in a heavy 4-quart soup pot:

3 cups water
½ cup rice

Lower the heat to a very low simmer, cover, and cook for about 20 minutes or until the rice is very soft. Put the cooked rice and any liquid still remaining into the blender or food processor with:

2 cups chicken stock

After the rice-and-stock mixture is well puréed, pour it into the soup pot. Open:

1 1-pound can salmon

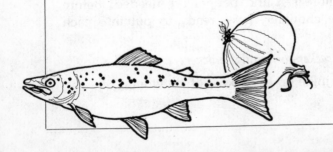

Remove any skin (you don't have to remove the bones) and put the salmon with its liquid into the blender or food processor with:

> 1 cup fish stock or clam juice
> 1 4-ounce jar pimientos, diced (including liquid)
> ½ teaspoon salt
> ½ teaspoon pepper

Purée the salmon mixture and then add it to the soup pot. Put into a small skillet:

> 1 tablespoon cooking oil
> 1 medium onion, peeled and finely chopped

Cook slowly over low heat, stirring frequently until the onion is soft and yellow. Put onion into the blender or food processor and add:

> 1 cup heavy cream

Blend well and then add the purée to the soup pot. Heat everything to a good simmer, then add:

> 2 cups fresh peas or 1 thawed 10-ounce package frozen peas
> ⅓ cup fresh dill or 1 tablespoon dried dill

Cook at a steady simmer, covered, for 10 minutes. Have ready:

> 3 hard-boiled eggs, thinly sliced

Garnish each bowl with slices of hard-boiled egg before serving.

Oven fish chowder

Because this soup is cooked in the oven, it needs less attention than many soups. Be sure that both the pot and the cover are ovenproof. Oven fish chowder is particularly delicious served *all'italiana*: over, or accompanied by, chunks of Italian bread, warmed for a few minutes in the oven. For a note on peeling tomatoes, see introduction to Italian red fish soup, page 100.

SERVINGS: 6 to 8
CALORIES: About 324 if serving 6; 245 if serving 8

Using a 4-quart ovenproof pot that has a tight-fitting lid, cover the bottom of the pot with:

   2 tablespoons olive oil

Arrange over the bottom of the pot:

   2 pounds boneless and skinless fish of any kind (fresh, if possible; but if frozen, thaw first), cut into filletlike slices

Pour into your palms, rub well, and then dust over the fish:

   ½ teaspoon dried thyme leaves

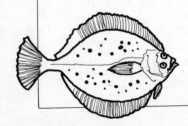

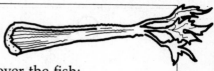

Arrange in separate layers over the fish:

1 lemon, peeled, pitted, and sliced very thin
1 medium onion, peeled and sliced thin
2 garlic cloves, peeled and sliced thin
2 stalks celery (including leaves), diced
3 large tomatoes, peeled and sliced
3 medium potatoes, peeled and cut in half lengthwise
  (don't cut any smaller)
½ cup coarsely chopped parsley (Italian parsley, if possible)

Dribble over this:

2 tablespoons olive oil
¾ cup white wine

Then add:

1 teaspoon salt
pepper

Next add:

6 cups water
1 tablespoon Worcestershire sauce

Put the lid on the pot and place in a preheated 375° oven for about 1 hour. Then remove the 6 potato halves with a slotted spoon and purée them in the blender or food processor together with a cup or more of the soup liquid. Put the purée back into the pot, break the pieces of fish with a spoon, and stir everything very well before serving.

On your own

To create your own soup, experimentation is necessary—and a little preplanning. After checking through the recipes in *Soup Wisdom*, you can see they call for diverse combinations of ingredients—leftover, on hand, or newly purchased. And if you review the chapter on turning stock into soup, you'll find lists of possible substitutes that are extensive enough to cater to most tastes. Also take into account the edibles you have in the kitchen. Then, if necessary, make a list of the other foods you may need in order to concoct a soup recipe of your own design. Remember—if you can make soup by following one of the recipes in *Soup Wisdom*, chances are you can also *create* a soup.

A rule to keep in mind when starting out on the adventure of composing your own soup is: for 6 to 8 servings you need about 6 cups of liquid. It can be a combination of stock and other liquids (water or liquid left over from cooking). The ratio of stock to other liquid will depend on the ingredients you plan to use in your soup. For instance, if you use dried peas, more water is called for. If, however, you use one 10-ounce package of frozen black-eyed peas, you might want to use less water or other liquid because as the peas thaw in the soup they will be adding water.

If you don't have the inclination to start with home-made stock, then buy it. But once you make soup with homemade stock you'll probably not want to depend on the store-bought variety.

You can use one of the recipes in *Soup Wisdom* as a basis for your own soup. Vegetable soup, for instance, almost asks for a personal touch. Toss in those scraps of meat you have on hand; why not try adding that leftover chicken; chop up those few spears of broccoli (cooked or uncooked); kernels from cooked or uncooked corn on the cob; chopped scallion tops; add a small can of peas, liquid included. The possibilities are nigh on endless. You just might happen onto a soup recipe to which you would be proud to give your name.

Who is to say, with Beethoven, that "only the pure in heart can make a good soup." But it can be said that a good homemade soup—better still, one of your own design—can express your knowledge and love of food as well as your imagination and ingenuity.

PART III

PART III

Canned soups

Condensed soup in a can was one of America's first real convenience foods. It was introduced by a small New Jersey company called Jos. Campbell Preserve Company. For a long while, Campbell and its early rival, H.J. Heinz Company, found the canned soup business slow going. Back around the turn of the century, few people were convinced that canned rivaled homemade. Sniffed the late Amy Vanderbilt, "In my own childhood, canned foods of all kinds were looked upon with great disfavor."

The Campbell Soup Company (its name was changed in 1905) worked hard to give canned soup a good image. In expensive advertising campaigns, the company plugged flavor and quality rather than convenience. Typical was a 1940 radio commercial in which the announcer rhapsodized over Campbell's relatively new cream of mushroom soup, describing it as having "a delicious, out-of-the ordinary taste . . . a blending of fresh, sweet cream, heavier even than whipping cream, and young cultivated mushrooms. Mushroom flavor fills every spoonful. Mushroom slices abound." Eventually, Campbell's campaign succeeded. In the American pantry, cans of soup—usually Campbell's distinctive red and white cans—became a staple. In the pot on the stove, canned soups took the place of homemade in many households.

True, today there's something of a backlash because of new interest in avoiding processed foods. The pot of homemade soup is once again bubbling in increasing numbers of American kitchens. Despite these trends, Campbell and its competitors still sell some $900 million worth of soup every year. It's clear that canned soup will remain a convenient low-cost staple of the American diet.

Campbell has a phenomenal 80 percent of the canned soup market, simply because it got into the business first and stayed out in front by spending plenty on advertising and by shrewd product development. The company has more varieties of soup than any other soup maker. (It has seventeen varieties of chicken soup alone, should you ever want to treat a cold.)

In 1976, Heinz, embittered by the failure of its "Great American" soups (a few of which Consumers Union top-rated in a report on canned soups in 1971), sued Campbell for monopolizing the canned soup business. Heinz accused Campbell of using "predatory" pricing and advertising practices to keep competition from opening up markets for new soups. The company charged that Campbell engaged in "the proliferation of brands of canned soup in order to acquire a disproportionately dominant position in the allocation of shelf space." The case was eventually settled out of court in 1979. Campbell continues dominant. Often, that leaves the shopper faced with shelves of Campbell's soups and few other choices.

Results of CU's tests

According to CU's tests, reported in the March 1980 issue of CONSUMER REPORTS, most canned soups don't taste very good. And most aren't very nutritious. CU tested fifty-seven soups of six popular varieties: chicken noodle, bean, tomato, vegetarian vegetable, vegetable with beef stock, and vegetable beef. CU bought soups made by Campbell as well as soups from Ann Page, Crosse & Blackwell, Progresso, Albertson's, and others. Of course, with the way that Campbell's soups predominate on supermarket shelves you might have difficulty even finding some of the other brands that CU tested.

Before testing the soups, CU had to decide on a standard serving size. The amount of soup that shows up in your bowl—and its cost and nutrient content—obviously depends in some measure on the size of the can the soup comes in. The vagaries of soup marketing, however, make such comparisons remarkably hard for consumers. If you add 10½ ounces of water to a 10½-ounce can of condensed soup, you get two 10½-ounce servings or three 7-ounce servings.

But what if the can contains 10¾ ounces or 11 ounces, or 13 or 8, as some did, or is of a type you needn't add water to? The different sizes don't provide a ready basis for comparison. CU eventually settled on an 8-ounce-cup serving for its evaluations. (In the recipes in Part II of this book, a serving is a 10-ounce bowl.)

The nutrients

Canned soups have been getting some sales competition from dried soup mixes (see pages 125–131). But CU found most of the mixes to be very low in nutritional quality. None would make a nutritious meal on its own. The canned soups CU tested were nutritionally better. Still, like most soups, none of the canned soups would make a nutritious meal by itself. To achieve that, canned soup would have to be eaten along with a sandwich and a glass of milk.

Canned soups don't provide as high a level of vitamins as a good homemade soup does. That's because canned soups are cooked at very high temperatures and pressures to ensure their shelf life over a long period. Those conditions, which you can't emulate in your kitchen, reduce the quantity of many of the vitamins originally in the soup. Generally available data confirm that canned soups are low in vitamins and minerals.

CU's investigations into canned soups also covered sugars and fat. Vegetables in these soups contained some sugars of their own; manufacturers added more. A number of the soup labels declare additional sugar, dextrose, corn syrup, or corn sweeteners. CU analyzed for total sugars. Results usually weren't dismaying— except with the tomato soups. A serving of those often had as much as 10 grams, or 2½ teaspoons, of added sugars. True, traditional recipes call for a dollop of sweetener in tomato soup. But 2½ teaspoons is no dollop. Besides, adding sugar hails from the days when tomatoes were a good deal more acidic than they are now.

In general, the soups were low in fat; that contributed to their rather low calorie count. Per serving, the typical soup contained about 2 grams of fat and some 60 to 70 calories. The bean soups tended to run a bit higher in fat and calories. (Calorie values were based on analyses by CU's contract laboratories.)

Additives

When testing dried soup mixes, CU found them to be a veritable chemical feast. Canned-soup makers, however, were nowhere near as prodigal with additives. But CU noted some additives: sodium, monosodium glutamate (MSG), and caramel coloring, among others.

There was enough sodium in many of the soups to give some people pause. Sodium is suspected of promoting high blood pressure and other conditions in some people. Doctors often put patients at risk on a moderate low-sodium diet. Such patients would do well to avoid all but the low-sodium canned soups.

MSG is a sodium salt used in many canned soups as a flavor enhancer. It induces in some people a condition called the "Chinese restaurant syndrome"—a variety of temporary symptoms that may include a burning sensation throughout the body, upper chest pain, facial pressure, and headache. CU found MSG in most varieties of the canned soups tested; but eleven out of twelve brands of tomato soup were free of MSG.

Caramel coloring is common in vegetable soups with beef stock. The additive is suspect since it's thought that caramelized sugar can form carcinogens. At this writing, the substance is on the U.S. Food and Drug Administration's priority list for testing.

Contaminants

Canned food can pick up lead from the seams in the container. CU's tests showed that most of the soups contained about 0.2 parts per million of lead—a level that's about average for most canned foods. CU also analyzed for twenty-two pesticides, and found no detectable levels of them.

Tasting the canned soups

For CU's sensory tests, all of the soups were prepared as their labels directed. When a label called for added water, bottled spring water was used. CU's sensory consultants compared each tested soup with an ideal homemade version of the same variety. In the version that the consultants used as a standard, all the flavors and seasonings would be balanced, with the main flavor predominating—chicken or tomato, say, or beef with vegetables. Only if a soup were comparable in all respects to the archetype would it be judged excellent. None of the fifty-seven tested soups made the grade, although four of them—three bean and one chunky vegetable—were judged very good. All of the rest were judged good, fair, poor, or variable—not a dazzling showing, although better than that of the dried soup mixes, most of which were judged fair or poor.

Chicken noodle soups

An excellent chicken noodle soup should have a clear, thin, pale yellow broth. Any chicken should be tender and in whole pieces, not in shreds compressed and cut to imitate intact chicken tissue. The chicken pieces should also taste and smell like real chicken. The noodles should be firm and smack slightly of wheat. Spices, salt, and sweeteners should be present in only slight amounts.

All nine of the tested chicken noodle soups fell short of such glories. Some of them had a distinctly tinny flavor. Salt had usually been laid on with a rather heavy hand. The chicken pieces, when present, were spongy, chewy, or hard.

Bean soups

The eleven bean soups were eminently successful as a group. The soups made with white beans looked white, as they should; those made with black beans were suitably dark purple-brown. Almost all of the soups were at least moderately thick and reasonably reminiscent of beans in flavor and aroma.

The black bean soups were very different from the white bean soups. Indeed, the white bean soups alone were quite varied; some were made with ham, bacon, or even pasta and cheese. There were a few defects. Some of the bean soups proved excessively smoky. Several purée-style soups turned out a bit lumpy or contained some bean skins. One was tinny.

Tomato soups

CU's taste experts looked for red or orange/red mixtures that were, at most, only slightly thick. They reserved their highest marks for textures that were smooth overall (though pieces of tomato and onion were acceptable). In flavor and aroma, they looked mainly for cooked tomato, with only hints of spice, salt, and tomato acidity; any sweetness in the tomato soup had to be quite understated.

On balance, the consultants judged the eleven tomato soups the least successful of the rated products. Most of the soups had a slow-dissolving, starch-thickened base that was detectable to the nose and taste buds. Other typical defects included excessive saltiness or sweetness, blandness, and a general imbalance of ingredients.

Most of the tomato soups were of the kind you thin with water and that was the way the tasters prepared them. Some of the soups, though, allowed you the nutritious option of using milk; the result was "cream of tomato" soup.

Vegetarian vegetable soups

Tomato gives vegetarian vegetable soup its characteristic color and, as matters turned out, much of its flavor. The rest of the flavor came from a mixture of vegetables, which proved reasonably good-tasting in most of the tested soups. However, the vegetables were softer in texture than CU's consultants would have preferred. Undue softness plagued the noodles in most of these soups, as well. By and large, the tasters judged the nine vegetable soups rather bland and very close to each other in taste.

Vegetable with beef stock soups

CU's tasters expected the beige, brown, or orange stock of these eight soups to smell and taste mildly of beef, mixed vegetables, tomato, and onion, with traces of spice and saltiness. The vegetables had to be cleanly cut and on the firm side. Most of the soups hit the mark reasonably well; CU's consultants judged all but two of them good. The only problems were soft vegetables and lack of beef character in some.

Vegetable beef soups

Judged by much the same standards as the beef stock soups, these nine soups had an extra component—beef chunks. The chunks did give these soups an extra measure of beefiness, but the chewiness of most of the chunks didn't make them much of an asset to the soups otherwise.

Recommendations

Canned soup is relatively cheap and convenient. But to CU's sensory consultants only three of the tested bean soups—*Progresso Macaroni & Bean, Campbell's Black Bean, Campbell's Bean with Bacon*—and one of the vegetable beef variety—*Campbell's Chunky Old Fashioned*—tasted about as good as a proper homemade soup.

Although canned soup may be all-American, it's not a nutritious meal. To get a meal's worth of nutrition you should eat canned soup with two other all-American favorites: a sandwich (maybe tuna, cheese, or egg) and a glass of milk. Or prepare a condensed soup with milk instead of water. Or stir an egg into the soup as it cooks, and accompany your meal with a slice or two of bread. Or simply eat the soup with a glass of milk and some crackers, and follow with a piece of fruit.

If you're making a meal of canned soup alone, you'll probably get better nutrition from one of the chunkier soups. They generally provide more protein and would probably provide more vitamins and minerals than the thinner soups.

Homemade soup, however, is the straight ticket to good taste and better nourishment. Admittedly, you probably can't can it. But you can surely make soup better than canned soup and make enough to last two or three days—and even longer—if you follow the advice offered in *Soup Wisdom*.

Dehydrated soup base

Soup Starter, a dehydrated soup base, was a relatively recent entry in the area of almost-convenience foods. As the TV commercial boasted, this product had "everything needed for homemade soup 'cept the meat." The Swift & Company product sells for about $1.40 per container, with six varieties marketed: chicken noodle, chicken rice, beef barley, beef noodle, beef vegetable, and ham and split pea. Consumers Union tested the chicken noodle and the beef vegetable types, and reported the results of its tests in the April 1979 issue of CONSUMER REPORTS.

The chicken noodle soup required 1½ pounds of chicken parts. To make the soup, CU food technicians placed the chicken in a large pot along with 7 cups of water and the *Soup Starter*, brought it all to a boil, and simmered for 1 hour and 30 minutes. (After cooking, it's possible for you to fish out the chicken, remove the skin and bones, and cut up the meat if you choose.)

The beef vegetable soup required a pound of beef, cut into bite-sized pieces. The beef had to be browned for about 5 minutes (an extra step the ads glossed over) before you added 8 cups of water and the *Soup Starter*.

Cooking time was the same as for the chicken noodle. According to Swift, one batch of either soup could feed five hungry people. CU thought five people might lunch on the soup, but it would make a Spartan dinner for that many.

Both soups made from the *Soup Starters* looked appetizing. The flavor was characteristic of the added meat. The noodles and vegetables had a pleasingly firm texture. The beef vegetable soup smelled a bit bland, but the chicken noodle was quite chickeny. Both soups tasted better and more natural than the regular dried soup mixes CU tested (see pages 125–131).

The soups made from the *Soup Starters* were also more nutritious than those dried soups—although much of the increased nutrition came from the added meat or poultry. CU's tests showed that the beef soup contained 364 calories per serving and the chicken, 273—with one serving equal to 12 to 14 ounces. (Calorie values were based on analyses by CU's contract laboratories.)

Like the regular dried soup mixes, *Soup Starter* contained a lot of sodium; the equivalent of about one-half teaspoonful of salt per serving. And, like them, it contained monosodium glutamate (MSG) and other additives. Of course, *Soup Starter* would not be as convenient as a regular dried soup, which takes just minutes to prepare. And it costs a lot more, when you add in the price of the meat or chicken. Still, it's more nutritious and tasted better.

Even more nutritious and better-tasting is homemade soup because of the limitless variety of natural flavors and nutrients you can combine. You can make your soup a personal statement—for there is practically no edible that has not been—or cannot be—used in making soup. And you won't get the additives you may not want. Be your own "soup-starter" and try some of the recipes and the various procedures discussed in Parts I and II of this book.

Dried soup mixes

Consider this: After the discovery of fire, soup may not have been far behind. Heaven knows, there was plenty of water around then, and archeologists have come up with stone crocks from prehistoric times. A bone left over from yesterday's hunt, a few leaves, maybe a little bark, and a couple of roots—*voilà!* Not up to gourmet standards, perhaps, but all natural ingredients, and on a bitter night in some wilderness, it might have just hit the spot. Well, civilization has made amazing progress when it comes to tossing a few of nature's gifts into a pot of boiling water. Or has it?

Consider this: dried soup mixes. These dehydrated soups are sold to people who think they don't have the time (or talent) to make the kinds of soups described in Parts I and II of this book. A dried soup mix is certainly convenient. If you can heat a pot of water, you can fix a dried soup. With a regular mix, you add powder to the water and cook. With an instant mix, you add hot water to the powder in a cup and drink.

How good are such short-cut versions of soup likely to be? To find out, Consumers Union tested forty-three regular and instant dried soup mixes for a report published in the November 1978 issue of CONSUMER REPORTS. Among the soups tested were chicken soup, beef soup, and a variety of vegetable soups.

Results of CU's tests

Judging by the labels, the vitamin content in the soup mixes was practically nil. A principal seasoning was salt, which some Americans could use less of, not more. The soups' flavor, which CU's sensory consultants did not find especially good, was usually dependent on monosodium glutamate (MSG), a sodium salt that causes unpleasant symptoms in some people.

The dried soups CU tested were lower in vitamins and minerals and higher in sugars than CU thought soup should be. Most of the ingredient labels indicated one or more (usually more) of the following sugars: corn sweeteners, sugar, dextrose, and lactose. CU analyzed for sucrose, or common table sugar. Some soup mixes contained no sucrose; most were fairly low in sucrose. The tomato soup mixes were higher than any of the other products, containing 2½ to 6 grams—about a teaspoon per serving.

Calories per portion were usually fairly low. The soup mixes in 6- and 8-ounce portions generally provided from 30 to 80 calories. The 15-ounce "noodle" soup mixes provided 320 calories or so—about what you'd get with a bowl of noodles. (Calorie values were based on analyses by CU's contract laboratories.)

Additives

The ingredients list on a typical dried soup reads a bit like the index to a chemistry textbook. Dried soup mixes are highly processed products. Their manufacturers use marginal amounts of food (dehydrated chicken, beef, vegetables, noodles), then add a battery of additives to make sure the product has some palatability and a long shelf life. On the labels of the soups tested by CU there were 125 different ingredients and additives. A dried soup mix might have dehydrated food ingredients such as chicken, carrots, parsley, onions, and so on. But it might also have salt for flavoring and MSG for flavor enhancement. It also probably has several formidable-sounding preservatives, consistency-improving agents, or flavoring agents, and it might have added coloring to make the mixture look more appealing.

CU's taste experts judged that saltiness was the major flavor characteristic of the tested soups. Salt is approximately 40 percent sodium. For the many Americans for whom high blood pressure is a problem, high-sodium foods such as dried soups should be used with caution. People on a moderate low-sodium diet should avoid the products.

Used in dried soups as a flavor enhancer, MSG may cause some individuals to experience what is called the "Chinese restaurant syndrome" (see page 117). All but one of the tested dried soups listed MSG as an ingredient. And even that soup included glutamic acid, the main component of MSG. Most of the soup mixes contained between 500 and 800 milligrams of MSG per portion. Some contained less. And some contained more than 1,000 milligrams per portion—about ¼ teaspoon.

Contaminants

CU analyzed the soups for molds. For many years, molds were considered innocuous. In the late 1970s, however, studies showed that many molds can produce potentially carcinogenic mycotoxins, or mold poisons. Only four soups of the forty-three soups that CU tested were entirely free of mold. The mold CU found wouldn't have grown as long as the product's package was intact. If the package broke, however, and moisture got into the mixture, the mold could grow. CU didn't know if the mold found in dried soups would have produced mycotoxins, but consumers shouldn't have to face that risk. The absence of mold in four of the soup mixes proved that some manufacturers were capable of producing mold-free dried soup. If some could, then all should.

Tasting the dried soups

How does this conglomeration of dried foods and chemicals taste after being immersed in hot water? CU asked its sensory consultants to taste the products. None of the regular dried soups was judged better than good; none of the instants was judged better than fair. Unlike good homemade soups, the dried soups contained few natural flavors, aromas, and textures. Some had artificial and "off" flavors. Most tasted very salty.

Chicken soups

An excellent chicken soup should have a clear, thin, pale yellow broth. A good cream of chicken should be yellow, too, but thick and opaque. Any chicken pieces should taste and smell like real chicken; any vegetable bits should be reminiscent of real vegetables. Chicken, vegetables, and any noodles should be firm. Spices and salt should be present in only slight amounts.

To a greater or lesser extent, all the tested chicken soups lacked the characteristic flavor and aroma of chicken. Although a few of the products contained tender bits of chicken, most contained pieces that were too chewy, too dry, too fibrous, or too few and far between. A few contained no chicken pieces at all. The noodles present were usually firm. Many of the soups were too salty. Many had the distinctly artificial flavor and aroma of bouillon cubes. Some of the cream soups were too thick and starchy.

Beef soups

CU's experts expected a beef soup to be beefy in flavor and aroma, brown in color, and only slightly salty or spicy. They wanted any beef, vegetable, and noodle pieces to be firm and natural in taste and smell.

With the beef soups, as with the chicken soups, the main problem was the lack of the characteristic flavor. Most of the beef soups tasted and smelled only slightly of beef, and some were entirely lacking in beefiness. Those that contained vegetables were usually lacking in vegetable flavor and aroma. Again as with the chicken soups, a good number of the beef soups tasted too much of salt and bouillon cubes.

Vegetable soups

A mixed vegetable soup should taste and smell like mixed, fresh vegetables, according to CU's consultants. Single vegetable soups, such as tomato or green pea, should have the characteristics of the fresh vegetable. Vegetable pieces should be firm, as should any noodle pieces. There should be only a slight trace of salt and spices.

Most of the tested mixed vegetable soups had only a slight vegetable flavor and aroma. Some tasted bland. A few tasted musty, or smacked of scorched or overcooked vegetables. Some contained only a few bits of vegetable, and those bits were often stringy. Some had vegetables that were nicely crisp, and noodles were usually firm. Many of the soups were heavy on the salt and the bouillon flavors. Most of the tomato soups had the character of dehydrated tomato—a slightly artificial taste and smell. They were often beady or grainy in texture. The green pea soups had a smoky, dried pea character and chalky texture.

Recommendations

CU believes that dried soup mixes do not have much to recommend them. Even the best of the tested soup mixes did not taste anything like homemade soup. True, most of the tested soup mixes were low in calories. But most were also low in nutrition. And most were high in sodium and MSG.

If you sometimes decide to prepare a dried soup mix, try making it with milk; the soup will taste better and be more nutritious, too. As for choosing among the soup mixes, you're on your own. No matter which one you choose, you'll get only so-so taste, low nutrition, sodium, and MSG. As an alternative to the dried soups, you might heat up a canned soup (see pages 113–121).

Or better still, if it's marvelous soup you want, why not try the real thing. And at the same time, have a little fun: Use your imagination, ingenuity, and your copy of *Soup Wisdom*. Parts I and II offer any number of hints and suggestions (to say nothing of outright recipes) for the makings of soups—thick or thin, hot or cold—and always nourishing.

Calories of some soup ingredients

	Volume measure	Approx. weight	Cal-ories
Breads and crackers			
bread, white, enriched (including French, Italian)	1 slice	1 ounce	62
bread, whole wheat	1 slice	1 ounce	56
crackers, oyster	10	¼ ounce	30
saltines	3	⅓ ounce	42
Cereals			
barley, raw	2 tablespoons	1 ounce	98
macaroni, raw	½ cup	2 ounces	202
noodles, raw	¼ cup	⅔ ounce	70
rice, instant, raw	¼ cup	1 ounce	116
rice, raw	¼ cup	1⅔ ounces	176
rice, raw, parboiled	¼ cup	1 ounce	114
spaghetti, raw (including vermicelli)	¼ cup	1¼ ounces	140
Cheese, cream, and milk			
cheese, cheddar	1 cup, grated	4 ounces	458
cheese, Parmesan	¼ cup, grated	1 ounce	110
cheese, Swiss	¼ cup, grated	1 ounce	104
cream, half and half	2 tablespoons	1 ounce	40
cream, light	2 tablespoons	1 ounce	64
cream, sour	2 tablespoons	1 ounce	57
cream, whipping, heavy	2 tablespoons	1 ounce	104

	Volume measure	Approx. weight	Cal-ories
milk, fresh, nonfat	½ cup	4 ounces	44
milk, fresh, whole	½ cup	4 ounces	81

Fats

butter	1 tablespoon	½ ounce	100
fat, beef	1 tablespoon	½ ounce	120
fat, chicken	1 tablespoon	½ ounce	126
margarine	1 tablespoon	½ ounce	100
oil, corn	1 tablespoon	½ ounce	126
oil, olive	1 tablespoon	½ ounce	124

Fish

anchovies, canned	3 fillets	½ ounce	21
clams, canned (including liquid)	½ cup	3½ ounces	52
cod, raw	1 piece (3 × 3 × ¾″)	3½ ounces	78
flounder, raw (also sole)	1 piece (3 × 3 × ⅜″)	3½ ounces	68
halibut, frozen	——	1 pound	454
halibut, raw	1 piece (3 × 2 × 1″)	3½ ounces	100
salmon, canned, sockeye	⅖ cup	3½ ounces	171

Meats (including chicken)

bacon, cooked crisp (1 ounce raw)	1 strip	¼ ounce	48

	Volume measure	Approx. weight	Cal-ories
bacon, raw	1 strip	1 ounce	156
beef, chuck, stew, raw	——	¼ pound	476
beef, ground, raw	——	½ pound	448
beef, round, stew, raw	——	¼ pound	294
chicken, raw, boneless	——	3½ ounces	151
ham butt, cured, cooked	2 slices (3 × 2 × ½")	4 ounces	246
ham, fresh, cooked	2 slices (2 × 1½ × 1")	3½ ounces	306
sausage, beef and pork, raw	1 link (2¼ × 1½" diameter)	2 ounces	252
veal, stew, raw	——	3½ ounces	346

Vegetables

	Volume measure	Approx. weight	Cal-ories
asparagus, canned	——	16 ounces	82
beans, green, raw, cut	1 cup	3½ ounces	32
beans, red, kidney, canned	——	16 ounces	408
beans, kidney, raw, dried	½ cup	3½ ounces	343
beans, lima, frozen, baby	——	10 ounces	345
beans, lima, frozen, fordhook	——	10 ounces	290
beans, lima, raw	½ cup	3½ ounces	123
beans, lima, raw, dried	½ cup	3½ ounces	345
beans, pinto, raw, dried	½ cup	3½ ounces	349
beans, white, raw, dried	½ cup	3½ ounces	340
broccoli, raw	1 stalk	3½ ounces	32
brussels sprouts, raw	9 medium	3½ ounces	45
cabbage, shredded, raw	1 cup	3½ ounces	24
carrots, raw	1 large	3½ ounces	42
cauliflower flowerets, raw	1 cup	3½ ounces	27

	Volume measure	Approx. weight	Cal-ories
celery, raw	8 stalks, 1 cup diced	3½ ounces	17
chick-peas, canned	——	20 ounces	1029
chick-peas, raw, dried	½ cup	3½ ounces	360
corn, canned, drained	½ cup	3 ounces	70
corn, cream-style, canned	——	16 ounces	372
corn, raw	1 ear	3½ ounces	96
cucumbers, raw	2 large	1 pound	46
eggplant, raw	2 slices, 1½ cups diced	3½ ounces	25
leeks, raw	3 to 4 medium	3½ ounces	52
lentils, raw, dried	½ cup	3½ ounces	340
mushrooms	——	½ pound	61
okra, frozen	——	10 ounces	111
okra, raw	8 to 9 pods	3½ ounces	36
onions, raw	1 medium	3½ ounces	38
parsnips, raw	½ large	3½ ounces	76
peas, raw, shelled	¾ cup	3½ ounces	84
peas, frozen	——	10 ounces	206
peas, raw, dried	½ cup	3½ ounces	340
peas, split, dried	½ cup	3½ ounces	348
peppers, raw	1 large	3½ ounces	22
pimientos, jar	——	4 ounces	31
potatoes, raw	1 medium	3½ ounces	76
sauerkraut, canned (including liquid)	——	16 ounces	82
scallions, raw	5	3½ ounces	45
spinach, frozen	——	10 ounces	68
squash, winter	——	3½ ounces	50
tomatoes, canned	——	16 ounces	95
tomatoes, ripe, raw	1 small	3½ ounces	22
turnips, raw	¾ cup diced	3½ ounces	30
zucchini (green squash), raw	1 small	3½ ounces	19

	Volume measure	Approx. weight	Cal- ories
Miscellaneous			
cornstarch	1 tablespoon	¼ ounce	29
egg, hard-boiled	1 large	——	88
flour	1 tablespoon	¼ ounce	29
honey	1 tablespoon	——	64
peanut butter	1 cup	4 ounces	1318
sugar, brown	1 tablespoon	½ ounce	52

The information for the ingredients listed in the table on pages 132–136 is based on *Food Values of Portions Commonly Used*, Church and Church, 12th edition revised, J. B. Lippincott Company, 1975.

Index

About Frieda Arkin

Frieda Arkin isn't sure whether to consider herself a cook who writes or a writer who cooks. She has published a novel, many short stories, poetry, and books on cooking and food. That she loves to write about cooking and food is not surprising, since she comes from a family of professional cooks. She has, she says, a particular reverence for soups.

Soup Wisdom is the first book Consumers Union has published with Frieda Arkin as coauthor. Her successful *Kitchen Wisdom* was published in a CU edition in 1977.

Paperbounds from Consumer Reports Books

Soup Wisdom
The basics of making soup from scratch, plus thirty recipes tested by CU. 1980. $4.50

Kitchen Wisdom
A kitchen book to make it easier when you cook, shop for food, and clean up. 1977. CU edition, $4.50

James Beard's Theory & Practice of Good Cooking
Cookery techniques, with recipes. 1977. CU edition, $6.75

Child Health Encyclopedia
A comprehensive guide for parents. 1975. CU printing, 1978. $7.50

Learning Disabilities: A Family Affair
How parents can help their learning-disabled child. 1979. CU edition, $5.50

The Consumers Union Report on Life Insurance
CU's guide to planning and buying the protection you need. Fourth edition, 1980. $5

The Medicine Show
CU's guide to some everyday health problems and products. Fifth edition, 1980. $5

Health Quackery
CU's report on false health claims, worthless remedies, and unproved therapies. 1980. $4.50

To order:
Send payment, including 50¢ per book for postage/ handling (in Canada, $1; elsewhere, $2), together with your name and address to Dept. SW80, Consumer Reports Books, P.O. Box 350, Orangeburg, N.Y. 10962. Please allow 4 to 6 weeks for shipment. Note: Consumers Union publications may not be used for any commercial purpose.